GMAT® STRATEGY GUIDES

0 GMAT Roadmap

1 Fractions, Decimals, & Percents

2 Algebra

3 Word Problems

4 Geometry

5 Number Properties

6 Critical Reasoning

7 Reading Comprehension

8 Sentence Correction

9 Integrated Reasoning & Essay

STRATEGY GUIDE SUPPLEMENTS

Math

GMAT Foundations of Math

GMAT Advanced Quant

Verbal

GMAT Foundations of Verbal

MANHATTAN PREP

Reading Comprehension

GMAT Strategy Guide

This in-depth guide takes the mystery out of complex reading passages
by providing a toolkit of sketching techniques that aim to build comprehension,
speed, and accuracy. Learn to identify the underlying structure of reading passages
and develop methods to tackle the toughest comprehension questions.

guide **7**

Reading Comprehension GMAT Strategy Guide, Sixth Edition

10-digit International Standard Book Number: 1-941234-06-2
13-digit International Standard Book Number: 978-1-941234-06-8
eISBN: 978-1-941234-27-3

Layout Design: Dan McNaney and Cathy Huang
Cover Design: Dan McNaney and Frank Callaghan
Cover Photography: Alli Ugosoli

SUSTAINABLE FORESTRY INITIATIVE Certified Sourcing www.sfiprogram.org SFI-00756

MANHATTAN
PREP

December 2nd, 2014

Dear Student,

Thank you for picking up a copy of *Reading Comprehension*. I hope this book gives you just the guidance you need to get the most out of your GMAT studies.

A great number of people were involved in the creation of the book you are holding. First and foremost is Zeke Vanderhoek, the founder of Manhattan Prep. Zeke was a lone tutor in New York City when he started the company in 2000. Now, well over a decade later, the company contributes to the successes of thousands of students around the globe every year.

Our Manhattan Prep Strategy Guides are based on the continuing experiences of our instructors and students. The overall vision of the 6th Edition GMAT guides was developed by Stacey Koprince, Whitney Garner, and Dave Mahler over the course of many months; Stacey subsequently worked with Dmitry Farber to execute that vision as primary co-authors and editors of this book. Numerous other instructors made contributions large and small, but I'd like to send particular thanks to Josh Braslow, Kim Cabot, Dmitry Farber, Ron Purewal, Emily Meredith Sledge, and Ryan Starr. Dan McNaney and Cathy Huang provided design and layout expertise as Dan managed book production, while Liz Krisher made sure that all the moving pieces, both inside and outside of our company, came together at just the right time. Finally, we are indebted to all of the Manhattan Prep students who have given us feedback over the years. This book wouldn't be half of what it is without your voice.

At Manhattan Prep, we aspire to provide the best instructors and resources possible, and we hope that you will find our commitment manifest in this book. We strive to keep our books free of errors, but if you think we've goofed, please post to manhattanprep.com/GMAT/errata. If you have any questions or comments in general, please email our Student Services team at gmat@manhattanprep.com. Or give us a shout at 212-721-7400 (or 800-576-4628 in the U.S. or Canada). I look forward to hearing from you.

Thanks again, and best of luck preparing for the GMAT!

Sincerely,

Chris Ryan
Vice President of Academics
Manhattan Prep

HOW TO ACCESS YOUR ONLINE RESOURCES

IF YOU ARE A REGISTERED MANHATTAN PREP STUDENT

and have received this book as part of your course materials, you have AUTOMATIC access to ALL of our online resources. This includes all practice exams, question banks, and online updates to this book. To access these resources, follow the instructions in the Welcome Guide provided to you at the start of your program. Do NOT follow the instructions below.

IF YOU PURCHASED THIS BOOK FROM MANHATTANPREP.COM OR AT ONE OF OUR CENTERS

1. Go to: www.manhattanprep.com/gmat/studentcenter
2. Log in with the username and password you chose when setting up your account.

IF YOU PURCHASED THIS BOOK AT A RETAIL LOCATION

1. Go to: **www.manhattanprep.com/gmat/access**

2. Create an account or, if you already have one, log in on this page with your username and password.

3. Follow the instructions on the screen.

Your one year of online access begins on the day that you register your book at the above URL.

You only need to register your product ONCE at the above URL. To use your online resources any time AFTER you have completed the registration process, log in to the following URL:

www.manhattanprep.com/gmat/studentcenter

Please note that online access is nontransferable. This means that only NEW and UNREGISTERED copies of the book will grant you online access. Previously used books will NOT provide any online resources.

IF YOU PURCHASED AN EBOOK VERSION OF THIS BOOK

1. Create an account with Manhattan Prep at this website:

www.manhattanprep.com/gmat/register

2. Email a copy of your purchase receipt to **gmat@manhattanprep.com** to activate

your resources. Please be sure to use the same email address to create an account that you used to purchase the eBook.

For any questions, email **gmat@manhattanprep.com** or call **800-576-4628.**

Please refer to the following page for a description of the online resources that come with this book.

YOUR ONLINE RESOURCES
YOUR PURCHASE INCLUDES ONLINE ACCESS TO THE FOLLOWING:

1 FULL-LENGTH GMAT PRACTICE EXAM

The full-length GMAT practice exam included with this book is delivered online using Manhattan Prep's proprietary computer-adaptive test engine. The exam adapts to your ability level by drawing from a bank of more than 500 unique questions of varying difficulty levels written by Manhattan Prep's expert instructors, all of whom have scored in the 99th percentile on the Official GMAT. At the end of the exam you will receive a score, an analysis of your results, and the opportunity to review detailed explanations for each question.

Important Note: The GMAT exam included with the purchase of this book is the same exam that you receive upon purchasing any book in the Manhattan Prep GMAT Complete Strategy Guide Set.

5 FREE INTERACT™ LESSONS

Interact™ is a comprehensive self-study program that is fun, intuitive, and directed by you. Each interactive video lesson is taught by an expert Manhattan Prep instructor and includes dozens of individual branching points. The choices you make determine the content you see. This book comes with access to the <u>first five lessons</u> of GMAT Interact. Lessons are available on your computer or iPad so you can prep where you are, when you want. For more information on the full version of this program, visit **manhattanprep.com/gmat/interact**.

READING COMPREHENSION ONLINE QUESTION BANK

The Online Question Bank for Reading Comprehension consists of 25 extra practice questions (with detailed explanations) that test the variety of concepts and skills covered in this book. These questions provide you with extra practice beyond the problem sets contained in this book. You may use our online timer to practice your pacing by setting time limits for each question in the bank.

ONLINE UPDATES TO THE CONTENT IN THIS BOOK

The content presented in this book is updated periodically to ensure that it reflects the GMAT's most current trends. You may view all updates, including any known errors or changes, upon registering for online access.

The above resources can be found in your Student Center at manhattanprep.com/gmat/studentcenter.

TABLE *of* CONTENTS

guide **7**

Official Guide Problem Sets

As you work through this strategy guide, it is a very good idea to test your skills using official problems that appeared on the real GMAT in the past. To help you with this step of your studies, we have classified all of the problems from the three main *Official Guide* books and devised some problem sets to accompany this book.

These problem sets live in your Manhattan Prep Student Center so that they can be updated whenever the test makers update their books. When you log into your Student Center, click on the link for the *Official Guide Problem Sets*, found on your home page. Download them today!

The problem sets consist of three broad groups of questions:

1. A final quiz: Take this quiz after completing this entire guide.

2. A full practice set of questions: If you are taking one of our classes, this is the home-work given on your syllabus, so just follow the syllabus assignments. If you are not taking one of our classes, you can do this practice set whenever you feel that you have a very solid understanding of the material taught in this guide.

3. A full reference list of all *Official Guide* problems that test the topics covered in this strategy guide: Use these problems to test yourself on specific topics or to create larger sets of mixed questions.

As you begin studying, try one problem at a time and review it thoroughly before moving on. In the middle of your studies, attempt some mixed sets of problems from a small pool of topics (the two quizzes we've devised for you are good examples of how to do this). Later in your studies, mix topics from multiple guides and include some questions that you've chosen randomly out of the *Official Guide*. This way, you'll learn to be prepared for anything!

Study Tips:

1. DO time yourself when answering questions.

2. DO cut yourself off and make a guess if a question is taking too long. You can try it again later without a time limit, but first practice the behavior you want to exhibit on the real test: let go and move on.

3. DON'T answer all of the *Official Guide* questions by topic or chapter at once. The real test will toss topics at you in random order, and half of the battle is figuring out what each new question is testing. Set yourself up to learn this when doing practice sets.

Chapter 1

Reading Comprehension

The Foundation

In This Chapter...

Chapter 1
The Foundation

Picture this:

> You've just received an email from your boss, asking you to review the Summary of Acme Company's annual report before the two of you go into a conference call with Acme's CEO. The Summary is six pages long and the phone call starts in five minutes.

The pressure is on! What do you do?

> (A) Speed-read your way through the entire thing. You won't actually remember or understand what you're reading, but hey, you did technically "read" it.

> (B) Start reading carefully, even though you're not likely to finish before the conference call starts.

> (C) Hand in your resignation.

> (D) Read the first paragraph carefully to get oriented, then start picking up the pace. Slow down for the big ideas, but speed up on the details.

The correct answer is (D), of course! You can't possibly read everything carefully in the allotted time, so you prioritize, looking for main ideas while minimizing the details for now. If the conversation does turn to a detail about one of those main ideas, then you'll have a rough idea where to look and can glance quickly through the summary to find the information.

Reading Comprehension (RC) on the GMAT is different from what you did in school, but very much like what you're going to need to do in business school. You often won't have enough time to read thoroughly and carefully—in fact, you may be given just 15 minutes to review a 20-page case study before your class starts to discuss it—so you're going to need to prioritize. This book will teach you how!

How Reading Comprehension Works

On the GMAT, you can expect to see four Reading Comprehension passages with three or four questions per passage, for a total of 12–14 RC questions.

The entire Verbal section will contain 41 questions that you'll have to answer in 75 minutes. That gives you an average of just 1 minute 50 seconds per question. In order to leave enough time for the questions, you'll want to read each passage in about 2–3 minutes, hence the need to learn a more streamlined way to read. The good news is that this more streamlined reading process will be immensely useful in business school, too!

The passages range from about 200 words up to about 350 words and from one to four paragraphs. Most people will see three shorter passages and one longer one, though this mix can change. The topics are fairly academic, covering areas in hard science, social science, history, and business.

The wide range of topics makes it likely that you'll like some passages more than others. Try to resist the temptation to dismiss any of the passages as "boring" or "not my topic." If you can convince yourself that the passage is interesting, you'll fare much better on the questions. We'll help you to develop this active reading stance throughout the book. In the meantime, keep in mind that you're not expected to bring any outside knowledge to the task—whether the passage is about municipal bonds or polypeptide chains, you'll be provided with all of the information you need to answer the questions.

The passage will always be on the left side of the screen and one question at a time will appear on the right, as depicted below:

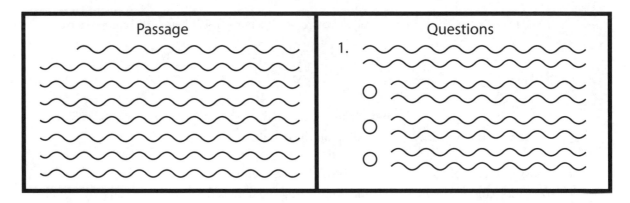

When you answer the first question, a new one will appear in its place. The passage will remain on the left-hand side of the screen. The GMAT will not tell you how many questions you're going to get; you'll know that you're done with the passage when the passage goes away and an entirely new question appears on the screen.

When you start to work through RC problems from *The Official Guide for GMAT Review*, you will see that the passages show line numbers down the side of the paragraphs. The actual GMAT exam does *not* number the lines in each passage. Instead, the exam will use yellow highlighting in the passage to indicate the location of a particular term, phrase, or sentence.

Find the Simple Story

Think back to the annual report challenge. You couldn't read everything carefully, or you wouldn't have been ready in time for the meeting. On the other hand, you couldn't just run your eyes over the whole thing or you wouldn't have learned anything useful from the text.

The challenge in situations like this is to find the **simple story:** the main points that you would use to summarize that annual report in just a few sentences for your boss. In order to do this, you really do need to read the text, but you do so selectively, paying attention to the main ideas while reserving the details for later.

Try finding the simple story in the passage below. This is a shorter passage, so give yourself approximately two minutes to read through the passage. At the end, you'll need to answer a couple of questions about the main ideas of the passage, so keep that in mind as you read. Take any notes that you like (or none at all—it's up to you), but resist the temptation to write on this page. Since the GMAT is administered on a computer, you will need to get used to taking notes on your scratch paper and looking back and forth between the two.

Bacteria

> Recent research into antibiotic-resistant bacterial strains suggests the need for a reexamination of the frequency with which doctors prescribe antibacterial therapy. One study demonstrated, for example, that most minor bacterial infections will resolve without treatment within 5 to 14 days of onset of symptoms; a course of antibiotics might reduce that time frame by only 1 to 2 days. A second study indicated that the incidence of "super-bugs," which have resistance to a wide variety of antibacterial agents, is increasing significantly and that these bugs are more likely to spread among those who have been treated with antibiotics within the past 5 years. In particular, researchers have become alarmed by NDM-1 (New Delhi metallo-beta-lactamase), which is not a single bacterial species, but a multiple-antibiotic-resistant enzyme capable of infecting other strains of bacteria.
>
> It is true that the proliferation of superbugs likely owes a great deal to the mistaken prescription of antibacterial treatment for viral infections, against which such treatment is ineffective, and to the routine addition of antibiotics to livestock feed in order to increase meat yields. Additionally, it is possible that ongoing research into the means by which resistance spreads among bacterial communities may lead to a new generation of antibiotics to which bacteria are unable to develop resistance. Yet these factors do not change the need for individual physicians to be more circumspect about drug therapy when treating cases of true bacterial infection.

Did you stick to the 2-minute time frame given? You have a little leeway (30 seconds or so extra), but resist the urge to spend much more time; the real test punishes those who don't manage their time well, and you'll build bad habits if you don't learn to work in the way that the GMAT requires.

1

Try the following two questions. Give yourself approximately 30 seconds for the first question and approximately 45 to 60 seconds for the second.

1.   The passage is primarily concerned with

   (A) discussing research into the symptoms of bacterial infections
   (B) explaining a change in the frequency with which antibacterial therapy is prescribed
   (C) contrasting the views of doctors and medical researchers with respect to prescribing drugs
   (D) questioning the routine prescription of antibiotics for bacterial infections
   (E) contending that physicians need to be more careful about distinguishing between viral and bacterial infections

6.   The research cited in the first paragraph suggests which of the following about antibacterial therapy?

   (A) It frequently leads to infection with NDM-1.
   (B) It is not generally used to treat minor bacterial infections.
   (C) It may help to reduce the incidence of "superbugs" that are especially hard to treat.
   (D) Reducing the rate at which such therapy is used would cause fewer bacteria to develop resistance to antibiotics.
   (E) Its short-term benefits, if they exist, may not outweigh the potential harm to the broader population.

The correct answers are (D) and (E), respectively. How did you do? These questions were testing your general understanding of the passage, so this is a good chance to check in and make sure you were able to come up with the simple story. If so, you were probably able to answer the two questions, as they mostly relied on a big-picture understanding of the passage. Question 1 tested this understanding directly. While it's true that question 2 did present some more specific material in the answer choices, the correct answer was not about the details, but about the author's main point.

Before reviewing the problems, let's talk about how to read the passage and find the simple story in the first place.

The first one to three sentences of a passage lay the groundwork for the entire passage, so at first, read carefully. Pay the most attention to the easier words that really tell you what's going on—not the technical ones that are just there to distract you.

Here's how a very strong test-taker might read the first paragraph. (The bold font represents text the reader pays close attention to.)

Passage Text	Reader's Thoughts
Recent research into antibiotic-resistant bacterial strains **suggests the need for a reexamination of the frequency with which doctors prescribe** antibacterial therapy.	*Hmm. I don't know much about "antibacterial therapy," but I know that "suggests the need for a reexamination" means something's not quite right about how often doctors are using it. Presumably the passage is about to tell me why.*
One study demonstrated, **for example**, that **most minor** bacterial infections will **resolve without treatment** within 5–14 days of onset of symptoms;	*Wait, so at least some of the time, you'd get better without even taking drugs?*
a course of antibiotics might reduce that time frame by only 1–2 days.	*If you do take drugs, they might not really have a huge impact. Interesting. Okay, so this might support the idea that doctors use antibiotics too much.*
A **second study indicated** that the incidence of "**superbugs**," which have **resistance** to a wide variety of antibacterial agents, **is increasing significantly**	*That can't be good. I know I've read stuff before about antibiotic resistance; I'm pretty sure it's not good.*
and that **these bugs are more likely to spread among those who have been treated with antibiotics within the past 5 years.**	*Yay, no weird words here. So these superbug things are definitely bad for people who've been taking antibiotics.*
In particular, researchers have become alarmed about NDM-1 (New Delhi metallo-beta-lactamase), which is not a single bacterial species, but a multiple-antibiotic-resistant enzyme capable of infecting other strains of bacteria.	*Uhh. Most of this makes no sense to me, but I get that NDM-1 is bad. It's also a detail, so I really don't care right now. Moving on!*

Right now, you may be thinking, "Wait a second—what if I get a question about that detail?"

The GMAT test writers create approximately five to nine questions for each passage, but you will be given only three or four of those questions. The passage will contain some details that you aren't asked about—and that might be the case for the NDM-1 thing. Do you want to learn about it just because you're very diligent and think it's the right thing to do, even if you never get asked about it? Of course not!

Don't waste time learning details that you might never need, especially when time is so tight. Rather, set the details aside for now. If you do get a question about NDM-1 later, you can find this text pretty easily and spend a little time working to understand it.

On to the second paragraph:

Passage Text	Reader's Thoughts
It is true that the proliferation of superbugs likely owes a great deal to the mistaken prescription of antibacterial treatment for viral infections, **against which such treatment is ineffective,**	*"It is true that"—it sounds like the author is admitting something that doesn't fit with the overall point.* *So these superbugs may be coming about because of "mistaken prescriptions"—they don't work for viral infections.*
and to the routine **addition of antibiotics to livestock feed** in order to increase meat yields.	*And another reason for superbugs …, this is just another detail, so I can speed up a bit. I've got the idea: it is true that there are other reasons for superbugs besides those given in the first paragraph.*
Additionally, it is possible that **ongoing research** into the means by which resistance spreads among bacterial communities **may lead to a new generation of antibiotics to which bacteria are unable to develop resistance.**	*An additional example …, is this following the same idea? Yeah, research might make the concerns in the first paragraph moot.*
Yet these factors **do not change the need for individual physicians to be more circumspect about drug therapy** when treating cases of true bacterial infection.	*Yet! We must be contrasting with the ideas just presented. I'm not sure what "circumspect" means, but it looks like the author is repeating the earlier point—doctors have to be more careful or thoughtful about prescribing these drugs so much.*

Here's the reader's simple story:

> *Something's not quite right about how often doctors are prescribing antibiotics. Two studies support this idea: 1) in some cases, the drugs don't really help, and 2) something about superbugs.*

> *There are some other causes of these superbugs—prescribing antibiotics for infections isn't the only problem—but it's still the case that doctors have to be more careful about using these drugs even for legitimate reasons.*

Notice how much that simple story leaves out. There isn't even a mention of NDM-1, let alone what it is or how it works. That's perfectly fine—if you get a question about it, you can go back to find the relevant text and read in more detail.

4 Steps to the Simple Story

Here's the basic process to find your Simple Story:

> **Step 1: Get oriented.** Read the first sentence or two pretty carefully.
>
> • Understand the topic under discussion and keep an eye out for any main ideas.
>
> • By the time you're done with the first paragraph, know the main idea of that paragraph. You may want to jot down a note. (You'll learn more about taking notes in Chapter 3.)
>
> • When a passage has multiple paragraphs (and they usually do), you'll probably read the first paragraph more carefully than any of the others.
>
> **Step 2: Find the main idea of each paragraph.** When you start a new paragraph, pay close attention to (at least) the first sentence. Find the main idea of that paragraph—why was it included in the passage? Again, you may want to note this down.
>
> **Step 3: Set aside the details.** When you get to examples or other very specific details, focus on *why* the information is present. Pay less attention to all of the nitpicky little details.
>
> **Step 4: Articulate the simple story.** When you're done, pause for a moment to articulate the simple story to yourself. If you had to give someone a 10-second summary of the passage, what would you say?

In subsequent chapters, you'll learn techniques to help you develop the simple story and set yourself up to answer both general and specific detail questions. For now, take a look at how this approach can make the process of answering certain questions easier.

Solutions: Bacteria Passage

Below are the two problems from the Bacteria passage. Now that you have a better idea of how to find the simple story, you may want to try the questions again before you read the solutions.

The first question is a primary purpose question; you'll learn about this question type in more detail in Chapter 4. The correct answer should convey the overall point of the simple story. Before reading the answers, remind yourself of that story. Then, eliminate answers that go too far beyond the story, that focus too much on certain details without conveying the main idea, or that actually contradict the passage in some way.

1. The passage is primarily concerned with

   (A) discussing research into the symptoms of bacterial infections

   Incorrect. The passage mentions only that symptoms can resolve without treatment; the symptoms themselves are not discussed.

   (B) explaining a change in the frequency with which antibacterial therapy is prescribed

   Incorrect. The author appears to be advocating a reduction in the use of antibacterial therapy, but nothing in the passage indicates that doctors are already prescribing this therapy more or less often than before.

   (C) contrasting the views of doctors and medical researchers with respect to prescribing drugs

   Incorrect. The first paragraph does present information that might seem to imply a difference of opinion between doctors and researchers, but the passage says nothing about the actual views of doctors or medical researchers. Further, the passage limits itself to one particular class of drugs; it does not address the prescription of any/all drugs.

   (D) questioning the routine prescription of antibiotics for bacterial infections

   CORRECT. Both the first and last sentences of the passage make it clear that the author wants doctors to be more careful about prescribing antibiotics. This fits the simple story: the first paragraph presents research to support this opinion, and the second acknowledges other causes of the "superbug" problem before reiterating that antibiotic use for infections is still an issue.

   (E) contending that physicians need to be more careful about distinguishing between viral and bacterial infections

   Incorrect. This is tempting. The passage does mention both viral and bacterial infections. Doesn't this mean that the author thinks doctors need to be careful here, too? Possibly, but the passage never says so explicitly. In any case, you don't need to get into that much detail to eliminate an answer like this on primary purpose questions. This answer choice doesn't address antibiotic therapy, which is central to the simple story.

The only answer that fits with the simple story is answer (D). Take a moment to look back: how might you have eliminated each incorrect answer quickly and definitively?

(A) Symptoms? Not discussed.

(B) What change?

(C) This passage is not about all drugs.

(E) Viral vs. bacterial? Not the overall point.

The second question asks about the studies in the first paragraph. Some of the answers are very detailed, but it's certainly okay to make a quick pass to look for an answer that matches the simple story. If nothing turns up, then go back and analyze the details.

2. The studies cited in the first paragraph suggest which of the following about antibacterial therapy?

(A) It frequently leads to infection with NDM-1.

   Yikes—I don't know! I skimmed the info about NDM-1. Come back later.

(B) It is not generally used to treat minor bacterial infections.

   They said it is used to treat minor infections—it only reduces treatment time by a couple of days. This one's wrong.

(C) It may help to reduce the incidence of "superbugs" that are especially hard to treat.

   I don't know. Come back later.

(D) Reducing the rate at which such therapy is used would cause fewer bacteria to develop resistance to antibiotics.

   I don't know. Come back later.

(E) Its short-term benefits, if they exist, may not outweigh the potential harm to the broader population.

   CORRECT. The paragraph does mention that such therapy might reduce the illness by one to two days. This could be a short-term benefit, but the author minimizes this benefit and goes on to discuss a much worse drawback (the superbug). That all fits with the simple story and the first paragraph.

It's sometimes possible to find the right answer even if you don't yet know why some of the wrong ones are wrong. On the real test, pick (E) and move on. When you're studying, go back afterwards to learn why answers (A), (C), and (D) are wrong.

1

(A) It frequently leads to infection with NDM-1.

> **Incorrect.** The passage does say that patients who have used antibiotics within the past 5 years are more likely to pick up these "superbugs," but it doesn't indicate how often this happens, especially in the case of NDM-1 in particular. Perhaps this bug is still very rare.

(C) It may help to reduce the incidence of "superbugs" that are especially hard to treat.

> **Incorrect.** This paragraph mentions nothing about what causes the incidence of super-bugs to decrease. In fact, the story hinges on the idea that these superbugs are *increasing*, so this answer contradicts the story.

(D) Reducing the rate at which such therapy is used would cause fewer bacteria to develop resistance to antibiotics.

> **Incorrect.** This is tempting! The question points you specifically to the first paragraph, though, and the first paragraph does not discuss what causes bacteria to become antibiotic-resistant. (The second paragraph does touch on this a bit, but it does not discuss how *antibacterial therapy* might contribute to this phenomenon—read the question carefully!)

In this case, the wrong answers weren't necessarily easy to eliminate, but the right answer was definitely connected to the simple story.

If the correct answer to the second question didn't match your take on the passage, you may not have read carefully enough. This typically happens for one of two reasons:

1. You read so quickly that you aren't really taking in what you're reading. Have you ever read something and then realized that you have no idea what you just read and you have to read it again? You'll need to learn to read actively on RC; purposefully looking for the simple story will help.

2. You get distracted by the technical words, the examples, and the minutiae; you're paying so much attention to those details that you forget to tell yourself the simple story. In this case, you're going to have to learn how to strip out the details and concentrate on the big picture.

As the book progresses, you'll learn techniques to help you overcome these (and other) problems by actively reading for the big picture and using that understanding to simplify the process of answering the questions.

Chapter 2 of Reading Comprehension

Breaking Down the Passage

In This Chapter...

Chapter 2
Breaking Down the Passage

Sometimes, you hit a passage that just speaks to you. You like the topic, the language doesn't seem as challenging, and you might even be somewhat familiar with the technical examples given. When this happens, go with it! Read the passage as though you're reading for pleasure and don't worry as much about building an explicit Simple Story. (Just be careful not to bring in outside knowledge.)

More often, though, you're not going to get that lucky. Remember the last time you started to read a passage and you wanted to groan aloud because you found the topic boring? Yet you still had to get through the passage and answer questions about it! What to do?

Engage with the Passage

The first step may seem minor, but it will be a real help. Think of someone you know who actually does like the topic. Pretend that you're going to tell her about it later: "Oh, Robyn would like this. I want to remember enough to tell her about it so that she can look it up if she wants." Who knows—you might actually discover that the topic isn't as boring as you thought.

Reading with your friend in mind, try to get enough out of the passage to be able to tell her (or him) a coherent short story. Lean forward a bit in your seat, smile, and do your best to convince yourself that you are reading this passage by choice and not just because you have to.

What do you want to remember to tell your friend Robyn? Certainly not some very specific detail four sentences into the second paragraph. Rather, you want to tell her the Simple Story. Having Robyn in mind will keep you focused on that task.

Passage Components

Do you remember what a thesis statement is? When you were writing academic papers in school, you had to include a thesis statement and provide support for that thesis. You were expected to have an introduction and a conclusion. In many cases, you were even expected to raise questions or acknowledge contrasting points of view, while ultimately showing that your thesis still held.

GMAT passages are, for the most part, excerpts of academic papers. They are much shorter, of course, so they don't contain all of the expected components of an academic work, but certain components will be present.

You do not need to memorize the different components, nor do you need to explicitly label every sentence that you read. If you know what to look for, though, then you'll be better equipped to find the Simple Story.

The Point

The point is the thesis statement: it is the single most important message of the passage and the heart of your Simple Story. The author has written the passage in order to convey the point, even if nothing else gets through to the reader.

Take a look back at the Bacteria passage from the last chapter. Where does the author express the point?

Recent research into antibiotic-resistant bacterial strains suggests the need for a reexamination of the frequency with which doctors prescribe antibacterial therapy. One study demonstrated, for example, that most minor bacterial infections will resolve without treatment within 5 to 14 days of onset of symptoms; a course of antibiotics might reduce that time frame by only 1 to 2 days. A second study indicated that the incidence of "superbugs," which have resistance to a wide variety of antibacterial agents, is increasing significantly and that these bugs are more likely to spread among those who have been treated with antibiotics within the past 5 years. In particular, researchers have become alarmed by NDM-1 (New Delhi metallo-beta-lactamase), which is not a single bacterial species, but a multiple-antibiotic-resistant enzyme capable of infecting other strains of bacteria.

It is true that the proliferation of superbugs likely owes a great deal to the mistaken prescription of antibacterial treatment for viral infections, against which such treatment is ineffective, and to the routine addition of antibiotics to livestock feed in order to increase meat yields. Additionally, it is possible that ongoing research into the means by which resistance spreads among bacterial communities may lead to a new generation of antibiotics to which bacteria are unable to develop resistance. Yet these factors do not change the need for individual physicians to be more circumspect about drug therapy when treating cases of true bacterial infection.

The point is encapsulated in the first and last sentences:

> Recent research into antibiotic-resistant bacterial strains suggests the need for a reexamination of the frequency with which doctors prescribe antibacterial therapy.

> Yet these factors do not change the need for individual physicians to be more circumspect about drug therapy when treating cases of true bacterial infection.

These ideas showed up at the beginning and the end of the simple story: *The frequency with which doctors prescribe antibiotics is problematic; doctors have to be more careful.*

This is the single most important idea that the author was trying to convey in writing the passage. If you can't articulate the point, or if you think something else is the point, you are probably going to miss at least some of the questions associated with the passage.

Your simple story will always contain the point. The point can be anywhere in the passage, but it is most often found in the first paragraph or the beginning of the second paragraph. Most of the time, the point will be contained in a single sentence, but occasionally you'll have to combine two or three sentences to get it.

What about the rest of the information in the simple story? Read on.

Support and Background

Some amount of the information in any passage will serve to **support** the author's point. This support is part of the story.

You may also think of some information as **background**: it doesn't strongly support the point, but it sets the context for information presented in the passage. Although this information does not strictly support the point, you don't need to distinguish background information from support—you can group it all together. Certainly, you wouldn't want to brush past a whole paragraph without understanding it simply because it looks like background. You need to understand enough of the supporting and background information to build your simple story, but you do not have to thoroughly comprehend or memorize how these details work.

Looking back at the passage, where do you see information that supports the author's point?

The supporting information is contained in the second part of the first paragraph: two studies support the point. In the simple story, these studies were crunched down to one sentence:

> *Two studies support this idea: 1) in some cases, the drugs don't really help, and 2) something about superbugs.*

The sentences in the passage contain a whole lot more detail than that, but it is enough to know that these examples support the point. If you are asked a question about any particular detail, you'll go back to the passage at that time.

Counterpoints, Acknowledgments, and Implications

2

Some passages will contain **counterpoints**, information that goes against the author's point (or at least appears to). Passages might also **acknowledge** a certain point or piece of evidence that does not support the point but that doesn't go against it either.

As with support and background, your goal is to know how the high-level information fits into the simple story, while leaving specific details for later.

Take a look at the passage one more time. Does it contain any counterpoints or acknowledgments?

The second paragraph of the passage begins by acknowledging that there are other possible factors (aside from the treatment of bacterial infections) that are contributing to the superbug problem. Nevertheless, the author eventually concludes that the original point holds: doctors have to be more careful about prescribing antibiotics even for legitimate purposes.

Whether you thought of these other factors as counterpoints or as acknowledgments is not nearly as important as recognizing that they did not ultimately support the author's point.

Occasionally, passages will contain **implications** for the future, answering the question, "So what might happen from here or what should we do about the situation?" The Bacteria passage does not contain implications, but you could imagine that the author might have discussed a need to fund additional research to establish that the over-prescription of antibiotics for bacterial infections is contributing to resistant bacteria. Alternatively, the author might have proposed a government panel to study how to influence doctors to reduce the number of antibiotic prescriptions. Both of those would be implications.

Use these components to help you find your simple story.

> **Step 1: Get Oriented.** Read the first sentence or two pretty carefully. Pay attention to big-picture, foreshadowing, or change-of-direction language.
>
> - Understand the topic under discussion and keep an eye out for any main ideas.
> - By the time you're done with the first paragraph, make sure you have an idea of the main idea of that paragraph. You may want to note this on your scrap paper.
> - When a passage has multiple paragraphs, you'll probably read the first paragraph more carefully than any of the others.
>
> **Step 2: Find the main idea of each paragraph.** When you start a new paragraph, pay close attention to (at least) the first sentence. Find the main idea of that paragraph—why was it included in the passage? Again, you may want to write this down. (You'll learn how to create passage maps in the next chapter.)

Step 3: Set aside the details. When you get to examples or other very specific details, focus on *why* the information is present. Pay less attention to all of the nitpicky little details.

Step 4: Articulate the simple story. When you're done, pause for a moment to articulate the simple story to yourself. If you had to give someone a 10-second summary of the passage, what would you say?

Language Clues

Sometimes specific language in the passage will signal important categories of information that will help you to build your simple story. Keep an eye out for clues about four big categories:

1. Big Picture
2. Foreshadowing
3. Changes of Direction
4. Detail

Big Picture

Big-picture language introduces or summarizes some kind of main idea. When you see words like these in a sentence, they should almost jump off the page. Don't get distracted by New Delhi metallo-beta-whatever. Pay attention to the main ideas!

Below are some common language clues that signal a main idea. When you see these, pay attention to the big picture without getting sucked into the details!

Signal	Implication
In general; To a great extent; Broadly speaking; In conclusion; In sum; In brief; Therefore; Thus; So; Hence; As a result; Overall	A generalization or conclusion follows
First, Second, etc.; To begin with; Next; Finally; Again	Two or more important points or examples are outlined (Pay attention to the overall purpose for listing multiple points; don't pay as much attention to the actual examples.)
X argues that; X contends that; theory; hypothesis	A named person or group holds a specific theory or opinion

Foreshadowing

When you watch a movie or TV show, you don't just passively gaze at the screen. You are actively engaging with the story, anticipating what might be coming: uh oh, she got distracted by the guy with the gun just as she was piecing together key arguments for the legal case—I bet she's going to make a mistake and mess up in court! Showing this distraction is a way for the director to foreshadow upcoming events.

Foreshadowing works the same way in writing: the author can drop a clue about something that he plans to say later in the passage. When you spot foreshadowing, you can use it to anticipate the point or other important ideas in the passage.

If you saw the sentence below in the first paragraph of an RC passage, where might the passage go next?

> Given recent company stumbles, it is important to ask: Is the potential return on investment worth the risk?

When an author asks a question in the beginning of a passage, she is almost certainly going to address that question in her passage. She may actually provide her opinion on the investment, or she may just discuss how the company should weigh the risks and rewards for itself, but some kind of discussion that addresses that question should follow.

How about this opener?

> For some time, government officials disagreed as to where to store high-level radioactive waste.

There are many possibilities for what immediately follows: perhaps the author describes the opinions held by different government officials, or perhaps he explains what caused the disagreement in the first place. However, it seems certain that by the end of the passage the officials will have come to an agreement. The language *for some time*, coupled with the past tense verb *disagreed*, indicates that the problem existed in the past but no longer exists today. The passage should tell you that the officials came to some agreement and determined where to store that nuclear waste.

Here are some examples of common foreshadowing signals:

Signal	Implication
Traditionally; For some time; It was once believed; It had been assumed	Contrast coming up soon; now, things are different
Some (people) claim (believe, define, attribute, etc.); It is true that	Acknowledge a valid opposing point
Statement of a problem or question	Possible fix for problem or answer to question (or statement that it can't be fixed or answered)
Current theory; conventional wisdom	New or different theory or idea coming up soon

The list above is meant to help you to start thinking about foreshadowing, but there are many possible language clues; don't just stick to that list. As you read the first paragraph, look for foreshadowing

language to help you anticipate where the passage might be going. The sooner you start to have an idea of the big picture and the point, the better!

Changes of Direction

Change-of-direction language can signal some kind of twist—a contrast or a qualification that could make for a good test question. In addition, twists can signal a counterpoint or a return to the main point.

In the Bacteria passage, the final sentence contains a change-of-direction signal:

> Yet these factors do not change the need for individual physicians to be more circumspect about drug therapy when treating cases of true bacterial infection.

The beginning of the second paragraph acknowledges some information that doesn't actually support the point. The appearance of the word *yet* signals that the author is about to change direction and jump back to that point.

Here are some common change-of-direction signals:

Signal	Implication
However; Yet; On one hand/On the other hand; While; Rather; Instead; In contrast; Alternatively	Indicate contrasting ideas
Granted; It is true that; Certainly; Admittedly; Despite; Although	Concede a point (author reluctantly agrees)
Actually; In fact; Indeed; Surprisingly	Indicate an unexpected result or phenomenon
Nevertheless; Nonetheless; That said; Even so	Assert a position after conceding a point
Supposedly; It was once thought; seemingly	Something appeared to be a certain way, but it really wasn't that way at all

Detail

Certain clues will signal that you should pay less attention on your first read-through. When you see these words, still run your eyes over the information, but change your goal: understand why the information is there, but don't try to understand or remember every last detail given.

Signal	Implication
For example; As an example; In particular; For instance	Provide an example
Furthermore; Moreover; In addition; As well as; Also; Likewise; Too	Add to something that was already said
Likewise; In the same way	Provide a new example or detail that goes along with a previous one
In other words; That is; Namely; So to speak; a semicolon	Restate something that was already said (in this case, you can use whichever set of words is easier for you to interpret!)

Optional Strategy: Breaking Down Complex Sentences

It is not unusual for a GMAT test-taker to read a sentence, pause for a moment, and think, "Huh? I have no idea what that means." The test writers are masters of the complex sentence, so it might be worth your while to take a few pages to practice in-depth reading on a sentence-by-sentence level.

You may or may not need this section. If you are a strong reader who often reads complex material for pleasure, then you have likely already developed your own techniques for breaking down complex sentences into simpler thoughts so that you can digest the full meaning. If that is the case, don't feel that you have to change what already works for you.

If, on the other hand, you can think of at least one "Huh?" moment while reading RC passages, then read on.

What does this sentence mean?

> In a diachronic investigation of possible behavioral changes resulting from accidental exposure in early childhood to environmental lead dust, two sample groups were tracked over decades.

At this point, you may be distracted by the word "diachronic." If you don't happen to know the meaning of that word, you have plenty of company! Believe it or not, you can ignore those kinds of words. When the test writers toss jargon words at you—scientific terms and the like—one of two things will happen. If you need to know what the word means, then the passage will give you a definition or a contrasting word that lets you figure out the weird word from context. If not, then the passage will just move on, and you should, too. Don't let one unfamiliar word prevent you from processing the rest of the material.

One way to move past such words is to turn them into single letters for ease of reading:

> "In a D investigation of possible behavioral changes …"

Here's how a reader might go about stripping that first sentence down to more manageable parts:

Passage Text	*Reader's Thoughts*
In a ~~diachronic~~ investigation of possible behavioral changes	*Someone was investigating behavior changes.*
resulting from accidental exposure in early childhood to environmental lead dust	*I don't know what environmental lead dust is, specifically, but I've heard that lead is supposed to be bad for kids. Okay, this makes sense: some kids were accidentally exposed to lead and someone then investigated some consequences.*
two sample groups were tracked over decades.	*Specifically, they investigated two groups of kids for a long time.*
	Okay, kids were accidentally exposed to lead, and somebody investigated two groups of these kids to see whether their behavior changed over time. *Hmm, I wonder whether the lead did affect the kids? Presumably, the passage will get into that.*

Here are the steps that the reader took:

Steps	Example
1. Break the sentence down into smaller ideas; ignore technical jargon.	The reader above read just one idea, then she stopped to understand that one part before continuing to read and add new information. She also ignored the word *diachronic*.
2. Make connections to things you already know; simplify complex language.	The reader didn't get flustered by *environmental lead dust*. Instead, she made a connection to something she already knew: lead is bad for kids. This knowledge went along with what the sentence was saying, helping her to wrap her head around the second part of the sentence.
3. Link to previous information.	As the reader understood each new idea, she linked it back to what she'd already read. At the end, she made sure that she had a handle on the entire sentence.
4. Anticipate.	Finally, the reader speculated about where the passage might be going. Such anticipation can help keep you actively engaged with the passage—even when the topic isn't your favorite!

As you might guess, breaking down sentences takes time. You won't be able to do this for every sentence in the passage.

Fortunately, you won't need to! First of all, you will actually understand many of the sentences just by reading them once. Second of all, think back to your goal: find the simple story. You don't need to understand every sentence. You only need to understand the sentences that present the big ideas—the ideas that will help you to find the story. When you get to complex sentences about examples or other detail, you can just read right over them and keep going.

2

Try another:

> While *Don Giovanni* is today widely considered Wolfgang Amadeus Mozart's greatest achievement, eighteenth-century audiences in Vienna—Mozart's own city—and the rest of Europe differed greatly in their opinion of a new work unexpectedly mixing traditions of moralism with those of comedy.

Passage Text	*Reader's Thoughts*
While *Don Giovanni* is today widely considered Wolfgang Amadeus Mozart's greatest achievement,	*While is a huge clue: contrast! I'm guessing that today is another important word: the contrast seems to be that DG is considered M's best work today, but maybe it wasn't in the past.*
eighteenth-century audiences in Vienna—Mozart's own city—and the rest of Europe	*There are some details about location, but the important thing is that this part talks about 18th-century audiences. As I suspected, it's talking about the past now, specifically about people who were there when* Don Giovanni *was written.*
differed greatly in their opinion of a new work	*They didn't agree—did they all think it was bad? No, it just says they* differed greatly *among each other: some liked it and some didn't. Wait, so what's the contrast?* *Oh, I see. Today, it's widely considered his greatest achievement. Back then, some people liked it and some didn't.*
unexpectedly mixing traditions of moralism with those of comedy.	*This feels like detail. If I get questions about why some people liked it and some didn't, I'll come back here.*
	The basic message: Today, people think DG is M's greatest achievement. In the 18th century, though, the opinion was mixed.

MANHATTAN
PREP

Problem Set

For each of the four passages below, take two to three minutes to read the passage and tell yourself the simple story. Then compare to the version in the solution. There are certainly many ways to convey the same content, but make sure that your version covers all of the big ideas of the passage.

Passage A: Animal Treatment

Over the course of the eighteenth and early nineteenth centuries, educated Britons came to embrace the notion that animals must be treated humanely. By 1822 Parliament had
(5) outlawed certain forms of cruelty to domestic animals, and by 1824 reformers had founded the Society for the Prevention of Cruelty to Animals.

This growth in humane feelings was
(10) part of a broader embrace of compassionate ideals. One of the great movements of the age was abolitionism, but there were many other such causes. In 1785 a Society for the Relief of Persons Imprisoned for Small Sums
(15) persuaded Parliament to limit that archaic punishment. The Society for Bettering the Condition of the Poor was founded in 1796 and a Philanthropic Society founded in 1788 provided for abandoned children. Charity
(20) schools, schools of midwifery, and hospitals for the poor were being endowed. This growth in concern for human suffering encouraged reformers to reject animal suffering as well.

(25) Industrialization and the growth of towns also contributed to the increase in concern for animals. The people who protested against cruelty to animals tended to be city folk who thought of
(30) animals as pets rather than as livestock. It was not just animals, but all of nature, that came to be seen differently as Britain industrialized. Nature was no longer a menacing force that had to be subdued,
(35) for society's "victory" over wilderness was conspicuous everywhere. A new sensibility, which viewed animals and wild nature as things to be respected and preserved, replaced the old adversarial
(40) relationship. Indeed, animals were to some extent romanticized as emblems of a bucolic, pre-industrial age.

Passage B: Higher Education

Critics of our higher education system point out the often striking difference between the skills students develop in university courses and the skills desired by employers. Stu-
(5) dents generally enter the university with the expectation that a degree will improve their job prospects, the argument goes, so why not give employers more direct control over the education process? Some commenta-
(10) tors have even gone so far as to suggest that traditional postsecondary courses be re-placed with short, standardized skills-training workshops.

However, the provision of vocational
(15) training is not the goal of most university programs. Rather, universities seek to pro-vide students with experience in a particular field of inquiry, as well as exposure to a wide range of disciplines and worldviews. Uni-
(20) versity students learn to situate themselves not only within the adult world of work and responsibility, but also within the broader streams of historical, social, and physical development that shape and are shaped by
(25) their actions and experiences.

It is certainly reasonable to ask whether this vision of education serves the interests of the roughly 2/3 of U.S. high school graduates who enroll immediately in
(30) 2- or 4-year programs after high school. Might some of these students' needs be better met by more narrowly-focused vocational programs? Current research suggests that, rather than serving as a
(35) reliable engine of social mobility, the U.S. system of postsecondary educa-tion can actually reinforce existing inequalities. However, it is not at all clear that a more employer-oriented
(40) system, in which immediate economic need might deter many students from entering academically-oriented degree programs, would be any more effective at producing opportunity for tradition-
(45) ally disadvantaged student populations. Further, it is worth considering that the kind of education traditionally provided by universities may confer benefits to society that are not as easily measured
(50) as an immediate boost in individual earnings. Before we make any sweep-ing changes on utilitarian grounds, we ought to consider the utility of the existing order.

Passage C: Rock Flour

Although organic agriculture may seem to be the wave of the future, some experts believe that the next stage in agricultural development requires the widespread adop-

(5) tion of something very inorganic: fertilizer made from powdered rocks, also known as "rock flour." The biochemical processes of life depend not only on elements commonly associated with living organisms, such as

(10) oxygen, hydrogen, and carbon (the fundamental element of organic chemistry), but also on many other elements in the periodic table. Specifically, plants need the so-called "big six" nutrients: nitrogen, phosphorus,

(15) potassium, calcium, sulfur, and magnesium. In modern industrial agriculture, these nutrients are commonly supplied by traditional chemical fertilizers. However, these fertilizers omit trace elements, such as iron, molybde-

(20) num, and manganese, that are components of essential plant enzymes and pigments. For instance, the green pigment chlorophyll, which turns sunlight into energy that plants can use, requires iron. As crops are har-

(25) vested, the necessary trace elements are not replaced and become depleted in the soil. Eventually, crop yields diminish, despite the application or even over-application

of traditional fertilizers. Rock flour, pro-

(30) duced in abundance by quarry and mining operations, may be able to replenish trace elements cheaply and increase crop yields dramatically.

Not all rock flour would be suitable

(35) for use as fertilizer. Certain chemical elements, such as lead and cadmium, are poisonous to humans; thus, applying rock flour containing significant amounts of such elements to farmland would be

(40) inappropriate, even if the crops themselves do not accumulate the poisons, because human contact could result directly or indirectly (e.g., via soil runoff into water supplies). However, most rock

(45) flour produced by quarries seems safe for use. After all, glaciers have been creating natural rock flour for thousands of years as they advance and retreat, grinding up the ground underneath. Glacial runoff

(50) carries this rock flour into rivers and, downstream, the resulting alluvial deposits are extremely fertile. If the use of man-made rock flour is incorporated into agricultural practices, it may be

(55) possible to make open plains as rich as alluvial soils.

Passage D: Pro-Drop Languages

In many so-called "pro-drop" or "pronoun-drop" languages, verbs inflect for number and person. In other words, by adding a prefix or suffix or by changing in some
(5) other way, the verb itself indicates whether the subject is singular or plural, as well as whether the subject is first person (*I* or *we*), second person (*you*), or third person (*he, she, it,* or *they*). For example, in Portuguese, which
(10) is at least partially a pro-drop language, the verb *falo* means "I speak": the -o at the end of the word indicates first person, singular subject (as well as present tense). As a result, the subject pronoun *eu*, which means "I" in
(15) Portuguese, does not need to be used with *falo* except to emphasize who is doing the speaking.

It should be noted that not every language that drops its pronouns inflects its
(20) verbs. Neither Chinese nor Japanese verbs, for instance, change form at all to indicate number or person; however, personal pronouns are regularly omitted in both speech and writing, leaving the proper meaning to
(25) be inferred from contextual clues. Moreover, not every language that inflects its verbs drops subject pronouns in all non-emphatic contexts. Linguists argue about the pro-drop status of the Russian language,
(30) but there is no doubt that, although the Russian present-tense verb *govoryu* ("I speak") unambiguously indicates a first person, singular subject, it is common for Russian speakers to express "I speak"
(35) as *ya govoryu*, in which *ya* means "I," without indicating either emphasis or contrast.

Nevertheless, Russian speakers do frequently drop subject and object
(40) pronouns; one study of adult and child speech indicated a pro-drop rate of 40–80%. Moreover, personal pronouns must in fact be dropped in some Russian sentences in order to convey particular
(45) meanings. It seems safe to conjecture that languages whose verbs inflect unambiguously for person and number permit pronoun dropping, if only under certain circumstances, in order to ac-
(50) celerate communication without loss of meaning. After all, in these languages, both the subject pronoun and the verb inflection convey the same information, so there is no real need both to include
(55) the subject pronoun and to inflect the verb.

Solutions

Passage A: Animal Treatment

In the 18th and 19th centuries, people in Britain grew concerned about the humane treatment of animals. This was part of a general movement toward more compassionate treatment of others. Industrialization also shifted people's views: in the new industrialized world, nature no longer seemed like a threat.

Passage B: Higher Education

University education doesn't always fit with what employers want, so some people think schools should teach more job-oriented skills. Universities want to teach more than that, but what would be best for students? Maybe the current system doesn't help everyone, but the author thinks the new idea is not necessarily better, and wants us to be careful about making changes.

Passage C: Rock Flour

Rock flour, a fertilizer made from powdered rocks, could provide a cheap source of nutrients for plants, dramatically improving crop yields. While some rock flour might be dangerous, most of it should be safe to use.

Passage D: Pro-Drop Languages

In "pro-drop" languages, the speaker often drops pronouns (I, you, etc.) because the verb form makes the subject clear. However, these two things don't always go together: some languages drop pronouns even though the verb doesn't indicate the subject, and some languages keep the pronoun even though the verb also makes the subject clear. The author thinks that some languages allow the speaker to drop the subject pronoun to accelerate communication.

Chapter 3 of Reading Comprehension

Mapping the Passage

In This Chapter...

Chapter 3
Mapping the Passage

You know how to read passages now, but you have one more skill to develop before diving into the questions. These passages are complex; even the simple story is several sentences long. You wouldn't want to take the time to write the story out, but it is very useful to jot down certain things. So, you're going to create a **passage map**.

A caveat: Your goal is absolutely *not* to take notes the way that you took notes in school. You aren't going to be studying this same passage again weeks from now; once you're done with the passage, you can forget about it forever.

Instead, your goal is to jot down just a few words that will help you to develop and remember your simple story (including the point) and to remember where in the passage to look when you need support on a question.

Why Use a Passage Map?

You're going to have to answer two types of questions: general and specific. The passage map will help you to accomplish two important goals:

1. Predict the answers to general questions.
2. Know where in the passage to find the details you'll need to answer specific questions.

The two goals above will indicate whether you're creating an effective map. If you can't answer general questions based on the information in your map, then you didn't learn enough about the big picture on the first read-through. You'll need to practice picking up on the main ideas and major changes in direction.

If, on the other hand, you *can* answer the specific questions based solely on your map, then you may have spent too much time diving into the detail on your read-through. Remember that the test will always include more detail in the passage than you will need to answer your questions; if you pay careful attention to all of it, you may run out of time on the test. If this is happening to you, you'll need to practice minimizing the attention you pay to details, possibly to the point of skimming some information.

Avoid relying too heavily on your memory when answering the detail questions. Remember, this is an "open book" test, and it is full of traps for those who are "pretty sure" they remember the details. Check the passage! If you form good habits and apply a consistent and efficient process even on the easier questions, you'll have a better chance to answer the difficult questions correctly.

3

Making the Passage Map

Your passage map is a written version of your Simple Story, but it will be heavily abbreviated. Your map should reflect the following info:

1. The point

2. The purpose of each paragraph

3. Any other info you would include in the simple story, by paragraph.

Every reader's map will be slightly different. You have the flexibility to organize in a way that makes sense for you. Of course, this makes creating an answer key to passage mapping a little difficult, but throughout this book, we will work to model the process in a way that provides guidance while leaving your own passage map style up to you.

Try creating a map of the Bacteria passage that you first saw in Chapter 1. Use any format you like as long as it reflects your simple story.

> Recent research into antibiotic-resistant bacterial strains suggests the need for a reexamination of the frequency with which doctors prescribe antibacterial therapy. One study demonstrated, for example, that most minor bacterial infections will resolve without treatment within 5 to 14 days of onset of symptoms; a course of antibiotics might reduce that time frame by only 1 to 2 days. A second study indicated that the incidence of "superbugs," which have resistance to a wide variety of antibacterial agents, is increasing significantly and that these bugs are more likely to spread among those who have been treated with antibiotics within the past 5 years. In particular, researchers have become alarmed by NDM-1 (New Delhi metallo-beta-lactamase), which is not a single bacterial species, but a multiple-antibiotic-resistant enzyme capable of infecting other strains of bacteria.

It is true that the proliferation of superbugs likely owes a great deal to the mistaken prescription of antibacterial treatment for viral infections, against which such treatment is ineffective, and to the routine addition of antibiotics to livestock feed in order to increase meat yields. Additionally, it is possible that ongoing research into the means by which resistance spreads among bacterial communities may lead to a new generation of antibiotics to which bacteria are unable to develop resistance. Yet these factors do not change the need for individual physicians to be more circumspect about drug therapy when treating cases of true bacterial infection.

Here is the simple story presented in Chapter 1:

> *Something's not quite right about how often doctors are prescribing antibiotics. Two studies support this idea: 1) in some cases, the drugs don't really help, and 2) something about superbugs.*

> *There are some other causes of these superbugs—prescribing antibiotics for infections isn't the only problem—but it's still the case that doctors have to be more careful about using these drugs even for legitimate reasons.*

Here's one potential passage map for this story:

① Problem: Doctors prescribe antibiotics a lot—too much?

    1. Sometimes the drugs don't even help!

    2. Superbugs $\uparrow$ = bad

② Other things cause superbugs, not just above

    BUT doctors still have to be careful about prescribing these drugs Ⓟ

The map reflects the major elements of the story. It clearly delineates the point Ⓟ. It shows what information is in paragraph 1 versus paragraph 2. It mentions the support and the acknowledgment.

This map wouldn't take long to produce, but you can certainly abbreviate more heavily, depending on how strong your short-term memory is.

Here's a more abbreviated version:

① Prob: Drs use antibio a lot—too much?

    1. Sometimes doesn't help!

    2. Superbug = ☹

② Other things cause superbugs, too

    But Drs still have to be careful re: using antibio Ⓟ

Someone with a great short-term memory and strong RC skills in general might abbreviate to the point that the map resembles hieroglyphics; only he or she would be able to read it. Here's an example:

① Prob: Drs AB too much

     1. ≠ help

     2. superbug

② Other → S, too

     Drs must take care w/ABs Ⓟ

3   Common Notations

You don't have much time to read the passage and make your passage map. The good news is that you'll only need your map for the few minutes it takes you to answer the questions. In fact, you may find that once your map has done its job and helped you to understand the passage, you don't end up looking back at it at all. With this in mind, don't try to create the kind of clear document you might study from in school; you can abbreviate very heavily.

Consider the following notations:

Tactic	Passage Language	Abbreviation
Abbreviate technical words or hard-to-pronounce names with a single letter, an acronym, or a much shorter version of the word.	serotonin Mihaly Csikszentmihalyi	S or sero C or MC
Use an arrow to show cause–effect or change over time.	Instability in interest rates can cause investors to avoid bonds.	IR unstable → ppl avoid bonds
Use a colon (:) to attribute an opinion or point of view to a specific person or group.	Many historians believe that economic interests can prolong a war.	H: $$ issues → longer war
Mark examples with parentheses or "eg."	A classic example is the behavior of the female sphex wasp.	eg S wasp
Use up and down arrows to indicate increases or decreases.	An increasing number of businesses are expected to reduce benefits for part-time employees.	↑ biz → ↓ ben part-time
Use math and science symbols that you already know.	greater than (or much greater than) less than (or much less than) change therefore	> (>>) < (<<) △ ∴

Problem Set

For each of the four passages below, take two to three minutes to read and map the passage and articulate the simple story. The solution will present written versions of both, but you do not need to write down the simple story.

Passage E: Redlining

In the 1960s, Northwestern University sociologist John McKnight coined the term redlining, the practice of denying or severely limiting service to customers in particular
(5) geographic areas, areas often determined by the racial composition of the neighborhood. The term came from the practice of banks outlining certain areas in red on a map; within the red outline, banks refused to in-
(10) vest. With no access to mortgages, residents within the red line suffered low property values and landlord abandonment; buildings abandoned by landlords were then more likely to become centers of drug dealing and
(15) other crime, thus further lowering property values.

Redlining in mortgage lending was made illegal by the Fair Housing Act of 1968, which prohibited such discrimination based on
(20) race, religion, gender, familial status, disability, or ethnic origin, and by community reinvestment legislation in the 1970s. However, redlining has sometimes continued in less explicit ways, and can also
(25) take place in the context of constrained access to health care, jobs, insurance, and more. Even today, some credit card companies send different offers to homes in different neighborhoods, and some auto
(30) insurance companies offer different rates based on zip code.

Redlining can lead to reverse redlining, which occurs when predatory businesses specifically target minority or
(35) low-income consumers for the purpose of charging them more than would typically be charged for a particular service. When mainstream retailers refuse to serve a certain area, people in that area
(40) can fall prey to opportunistic smaller retailers who sell inferior goods at higher prices.

Passage F: Tokugawa

The Tokugawa period in Japan (1603–1867) serves as a laboratory for organizational behavior historians for the same reason that Iceland is an ideal location for geneticists—
(5) isolation removes extraneous variables. The Tokugawa shoguns brought peace to a land of warring feudal lords. To preserve that tranquility, the Tokugawa shogunate forbade contact with the outside world, allowing
(10) only a few Dutch trading ships to dock at one restricted port. Domestically, in pursuit of the same goal, the social order was fixed; there were four classes—warriors [samurai], artisans, merchants, and farmers or peasants—and
(15) social mobility was prohibited. The ensuing stability and peace brought a commercial prosperity that lasted nearly two hundred years.

However, as psychologists and social
(20) historians have observed, in varying ways, humans often fail to anticipate unintended consequences. In the Tokugawa period, the fixed social hierarchy placed the samurai on top; they and the government
(25) were essentially supported by levies on the peasantry, as the other two classes were demographically and economically inconsequential. However, prosperity brought riches to the commercial classes
(30) and their numbers burgeoned. Eventually, their economic power dwarfed that of their supposed superiors, the samurai, but the social structure was so ingrained that it was unthinkable to
(35) change. By the early nineteenth century, this imbalance between social structure and economic reality eroded the stability of the society. This condition was one of the primary factors that led to the
(40) eventual collapse of the shogunate in 1867. In short, the success of the self-imposed order led to its undoing through consequences that were beyond the ken of the founders.

Passage G: Prescription Errors

In Europe, medical prescriptions were histori-
cally written in Latin. A prescription for eye
drops written in Amsterdam could be filled
in Paris, because the abbreviation *OS* meant
(5)   "left eye" in both places. With the disappear-
ance of Latin as a lingua franca, however, abbreviations such as *OS* can easily be confused
with *AS* (left ear) or *per os* (by mouth), even
by trained professionals. Misinterpretations
(10) of medical instructions can be fatal. In the
early 1990s, two infants died in separate but
identical tragedies: they were each administered 5 milligrams of morphine, rather than
0.5 milligrams, as the dosage was written
(15) without an initial zero. The naked decimal (.5)
was subsequently misread.

The personal and economic costs of
misinterpreted medical prescriptions and
instructions are hard to quantify. How-
(20) ever, anecdotal evidence suggests that
misinterpretations are prevalent. While
mistakes will always happen in any human
endeavor, medical professionals, hospital
administrators, and policymakers should
(25) continually work to drive the prescription
error rate to zero, taking simple correc-
tive steps and also pushing for additional
investments.

Certain measures are widely agreed
(30) upon but may be difficult to enforce, given
the decentralization of the healthcare system
in the United States. For instance, profes-
sional organizations have publicly advocated
against the use of Latin abbreviations
(35) and other relics of historical pharmacol-
ogy. As a result, incidents in which *qd*
(every day) and *qid* (four times a day)
have been mixed up seem to be on the
decline. Other measures have been taken
(40) by regulators. For instance, the Federal
Drug Administration asked a manufac-
turer to change the name of Losec, an
antacid, to Prilosec, so that confusion
with Lasix, a diuretic, would be reduced.
(45) Unfortunately, there have been at least
a dozen reports of accidental switches
between Prilosec and Prozac, an anti-
depressant. As more drugs reach the
market, drug-name "traffic control" will
(50) only become more complicated.

Other measures are controversial
or require significant investment. For
instance, putting the patient's condition
on the prescription would allow double-
(55) checking but also compromise patient
privacy. Computerized prescriber order
entry (CPOE) systems seem to fix the in-
famous problem of illegible handwriting,
but many CPOE systems permit naked
(60) decimals and other dangerous practices.
Moreover, since fallible humans must still
enter and retrieve the data, any techno-
logical fixes must be accompanied by
substantial training. Ultimately, a multi-
(65) pronged approach is needed to address
the issue.

3

Passage H: Ether's Existence

In 1887, an ingenious experiment performed by Albert Michelson and Edward Morley severely undermined classical physics by failing to confirm the existence of "ether," a
(5) ghostly massless medium that was thought to permeate the universe. This finding had profound results, ultimately paving the way for acceptance of Einstein's special theory of relativity.

(10) Prior to the Michelson–Morley experiment, nineteenth-century physics conceived of light as a wave propagated at constant speed through the ether. The existence of ether was hypothesized in part to explain
(15) the transmission of light, which was believed to be impossible through "empty" space. Physical objects, such as planets, were also thought to glide frictionlessly through the unmoving ether.

(20) The Michelson–Morley experiment relied on the fact that the Earth, which orbits the Sun, would have to be in motion relative to a fixed ether. Just as a person on a motorcycle experiences a "wind" caused by her own
(25) motion relative to the air, the Earth would experience an "ethereal wind" caused by its motion through the ether. Such a wind would affect our measurements of the speed of light. If the speed of light is fixed
(30) with respect to the ether, but the earth is moving through the ether, then to an observer on Earth light must appear to move faster in a "downwind" direction than in an "upwind" direction.

(35) In 1887 there were no clocks sufficiently precise to detect the speed differences that would result from an ethereal wind. Michelson and Morley surmounted this problem by using the
(40) wavelike properties of light itself to test for such speed differences. In their apparatus, known as an "interferometer," a single beam of light is split in half. Mirrors guide each half of the beam along a
(45) separate trajectory before ultimately reuniting the two half-beams into a single beam. If one half-beam has moved more slowly than the other, the reunited beams will be out of phase with each
(50) other. In other words, peaks of the first half-beam will not coincide exactly with peaks of the second half-beam, resulting in an interference pattern in the reunited beam. Michelson and Morley detected
(55) only a tiny degree of interference in the reunited light beam—far less than what was expected based on the motion of the Earth.

Solutions

The solutions present one version of a passage map, but your version will likely vary. The solutions also include simple stories, but you don't need to write these down when you are working a passage—the passage map should be enough to allow you to put together the simple story.

Passage E: Redlining

Passage map:

1. Redlining: deny/limit service to minorities
2. Now illegal, but still happens
3. Leads to reverse redlining: charging more than typical

Simple story:

Redlining is denying or limiting services to minority customers. It's been illegal since the late '60s but some businesses still do it. It can also lead to reverse redlining, where businesses do offer service to the minority communities, but at a higher price than they would typically charge.

Passage F: Tokugawa

Passage map:

1. T isolated; fixed social order; peace/stable.
2. BUT merchants → wealthy, messed up social order, system collapsed. Fixed soc. order helped and hurt

Simple story:

The T period in Japan is good to study because it was isolated. The social order was fixed and they had a really stable era. Later, a "lower" group became wealthy, but the rigid social system stayed. So what helped make things stable at first eventually caused the system to collapse.

Passage G: Prescription Errors

Passage map:

1. Eur. Rx in Latin, but now confusing; errors dangerous
2. DK how much error, but maybe lots. Try to ↓
3. Pop. measures: no Latin, no similar names
4. Other measures controv.: listing condition, computers

Simple story:

> There are many ways to misinterpret medical prescriptions, and this can be dangerous. Some measures—such as eliminating the use of Latin and making names unambiguous—are agreed upon, but others are more controversial.

Passage H: Ether's Existence

Passage map:

1. 1887, M&M—no ether; made way for Einstein
2. Before, ether explained how light moved
3. Basis for exp: ether should affect meas. of light speed
4. M&M split light: no interference, no ether

Simple story:

> Prior to 1887, scientists thought that space was not "empty," but filled with a substance called ether. In 1887, Michelson and Morley conducted an experiment that involved splitting a beam of light. There was less interference than there should have been if ether existed, so the experiment did not confirm the existence of ether.

Chapter 4

of

Reading Comprehension

General Questions

In This Chapter...

Chapter 4
General Questions

Reading Comprehension questions can be grouped into two major categories:

General questions: Primary Purpose, Paragraph

Specific questions: Detail, Inference, Specific Purpose

This chapter will cover **general questions**, which may ask you about the overall purpose of the passage or about the purpose of a specific paragraph. The next chapter will cover specific question types.

You won't see more than one general question per passage; in fact, on some passages you won't see any. On average, expect to spend 30–60 seconds on each general question.

Four Steps to the Answer

In this chapter, you'll learn how to answer primary purpose and **paragraph** questions using a standard four-step process that you'll use for all RC questions.

Step 1: Identify the question. This chapter will tell you how to recognize that you have a primary purpose or a paragraph question.

Step 2: Find the support. If you have read through the passage effectively, then you should have a strong idea of the overall point and the purpose of each paragraph without having to go back to the passage. At most, you'll take a look at your passage map; you may also just know the necessary information already. (Note: On specific questions, you *will* have to go back to the passage—more on this in the next chapter.)

Step 3: Predict an answer. Take a look at the question again and, using your map or memory, try to formulate a rough answer in your own words.

Step 4: Eliminate and find a match. Evaluate each answer, while keeping in mind your predicted answer. When you find a potential match, leave it in and continue to eliminate.

- If you eliminate four answers, great! Pick the remaining one and move on.

- If you still have two or three answers left, compare the answers to the relevant information in the passage. If the answers are very similar, you may also compare them to each other.

- If you still have four or five answers left, make sure you are answering the right question! After that, it's probably best to cut your losses: guess and move on.

Finally, one last word of advice. This might seem obvious, but *every single word* in the answer choice must be supported in order for that choice to be correct. Make sure that you are reading methodically. Don't rush just because you're stressed; saving 10 seconds is not worth the risk of missing a question due to a careless mistake!

Practice Passage: Insect Behavior

Give yourself approximately four minutes to read the passage below and answer the questions that follow.

At times, insect behavior appears to be explicable in terms of unconscious stimulus-response mechanisms; when scrutinized, it often reveals a stereotyped, inflexible
(5) quality. A classic series of experiments were performed on the female sphex wasp. The mother leaves her egg sealed in a burrow alongside a paralyzed grasshopper or other insect, which her larva can eat when it
(10) hatches. Typically, before she deposits the grasshopper in the burrow, she leaves it at the entrance and goes inside to inspect the burrow. If the inspection reveals no problems, she drags the grasshopper inside by
(15) its antennae. Once the larvae hatch, they feed on the paralyzed insects until ready to spin a cocoon and undergo metamorphosis.

Entomologist Jean-Henri Fabre discovered that if the grasshopper's antennae are
(20) removed while the wasp is inside inspecting the nest, the wasp will not drag it into the burrow, even though the legs or ovipositor could serve the same function as the antennae. Later Fabre found
(25) more evidence of the wasp's dependence on predetermined routine. While a wasp was performing her inspection of a burrow, he moved the grasshopper a few centimeters away from the burrow's
(30) mouth. The wasp brought the grasshopper back to the edge of the burrow, then began a whole new inspection. When Fabre took this opportunity to move the food again, the wasp repeated her
(35) routine. Fabre performed his disruptive maneuver forty times, and the wasp's response never changed.

1. The primary purpose of the passage is to

    (A) demonstrate, based on examples, that insects lack awareness of their surroundings

    (B) argue that insects are unique in their dependence on rigid routines

    (C) analyze the maternal behavior of wasps

    (D) contrast typical wasp behavior with unconscious behavior

    (E) contend that insect behavior can rely on rigid routines that appear to be unconscious

2. Which of the following best describes the purpose of the second paragraph of the passage?

    (A) To provide experimental evidence for the thesis articulated in the first paragraph

    (B) To introduce a hypothesis about insect behavior

    (C) To illustrate the ways in which grasshoppers are unsuitable for the wasp's purposes

    (D) To explore the significance of the wasp's varied reactions to certain stimuli

    (E) To acknowledge experimental evidence that does not support the author's thesis

Here's one example of a simple story, with the point noted:

The point → *Insect behavior is sometimes inflexible or unconscious. Normally, a wasp inspects the burrow, then brings the grasshopper inside, and later the larvae feed on the grasshopper.*

Fabre discovered that the wasp will only *drag a grasshopper by the antennae. He also found that, if the grasshopper is moved during the inspection phase, then the wasp will put the grasshopper back and inspect again, over and over.*

Hmm. That sounds pretty inflexible—it's as though it can't think or adapt.

That last line is not stated in the passage, but a reader might summarize the idea in this way.

Here's one example of a passage map:

① Insects: behavior inflex, unconsc
    Typ: wasp inspect burrow, bring grasshopper, larvae eat

② Fabre: wasp will ONLY drag by antennae
    If grasshopper moves, wasp re-inspects burrow, every time.

Here's a more abbreviated version:

① Insect: inflex
    Normal W

② F: ONLY ant.
    inspect

The second map is so abbreviated that it serves only as a quick reminder of things that the reader already remembers: the normal behavior is described in the first paragraph, the second paragraph has that inspection example, and so on. If your short-term memory is strong, then feel free to use a hyper-abbreviated Map like this one. (You might not even write anything at all, but only follow that path if you can maintain a strong mental sense of the passage throughout the process of reading and answering the questions.)

Primary Purpose Questions

Step 1 on any question is to **identify the question type**.

    1. The primary purpose of the passage is to

This is a primary purpose question—the test writers are asking for the point of the whole passage.

Most of the time, these questions will ask you to identify the "primary purpose" of the passage or what the author is "primarily concerned with." The correct answer should fit with the point that you have articulated to yourself.

Steps 2 and 3 merge for primary purpose questions: **find the support** and **predict an answer**. For primary purpose questions, you don't need to go back to the passage. You should already have identified the point—if not, briefly review your map. In this passage, the point is that some insect behaviors seem to be inflexible; the insects can't adapt to changing situations.

Once you have that set in your head, it's time for Step 4: **eliminate and find a match**. For primary purpose questions, eliminate any choice that doesn't match the point. For example:

(A) demonstrate, based on examples, that insects lack awareness of their surroundings	*The insect is clearly aware—she sees that the grasshopper has moved and she goes and gets it. The point is about insects' unconscious behavior, not their general awareness.*
(B) argue that insects are unique in their dependence on rigid routines	*The author does argue that insects are dependent on rigid routines but never claims that they are* unique *in this way.*
(C) analyze the maternal behavior of wasps	*The author uses a couple of examples of wasp behavior to make a more general point about insect behavior.*
(D) contrast typical wasp behavior with unconscious behavior	*The author does not present* typical behavior *and* unconscious behavior *as different things. Rather, the typical behavior never changes, even when a disruption of the routine would seem to warrant changing a behavior.*
(E) contend that insect behavior can rely on rigid routines that appear to be unconscious	**CORRECT.** *The author claims that, at times,* insect behavior *is* inflexible, *or rigid, and the insect does not appear capable of responding to an unexpected or changed situation.*

Several types of trap answers appeared in this question.

One word off: These trap answers mostly look good, but one word isn't supported by the passage, taking the answer choice out of contention. Answer (B) was one word off. (Note: this can stretch to two words off!)

Extreme: These trap answers contain an extreme word, such as *all* or *never,* that is not supported by the passage. It is certainly possible for extreme words to appear in a correct answer, but only if the passage provides direct support for such extreme language. Answer (B) contained an extreme word (*unique*) that was not supported by the passage (that word was also the one word off—categories can sometimes overlap!).

Out of Scope: These trap answers will typically touch on aspects of the passage, but will go further than what the passage actually discusses. Sometimes, these answers are just a bit too broad; other times, they are way off. Answer (A) talks about *awareness of their surroundings,* which isn't discussed in the passage.

True but not right: These answers will typically reflect things that are true according to the passage, but they do not answer the specific question asked. Answer (C) falls into this category. The examples used in the passage *are* about maternal wasp behavior, but the overall point is about a broader topic: the inflexible nature of insect behavior in general.

Direct contradiction: Answer (D) is an example of a direct contradiction: the passage actually says the opposite of what this answer choice conveys.

4

Paragraph Questions

In order to answer paragraph questions correctly, you will need to have a strong grasp of the point of the passage as well as the purpose of each paragraph.

Most of the time, Paragraph questions will ask you for one of two things: 1) the purpose of a particular paragraph in the context of the whole passage, or 2) the purpose of a particular paragraph in relation to another particular paragraph.

First, identify the question.

2. Which of the following best describes the purpose of the second paragraph of the passage?

In this case, the question asks for the purpose of the second paragraph in the context of the entire passage.

Second, find the support. Locate paragraph 2 in your map:

① Insects: behavior inflex, unconsc
      Typ: wasp inspect burrow, bring grasshopper, larvae eat

② Fabre: wasp will ONLY drag by antennae
      If grasshopper moves, wasp re-inspects burrow, every time

Third, predict an answer. The second paragraph provides examples that support the overall point that insect behavior is inflexible.

Once you have that set in your head, eliminate and find a match. For paragraph questions, try to disprove each answer. If the answer contains something that wasn't part of the passage, or was restricted to a different paragraph, cross it off.

Before you look at the explanations below, try to label some of the wrong answers using the trap categories you learned on the last problem.

(A) To provide experimental evidence for the thesis articulated in the first paragraph	**CORRECT.** *The second paragraph does talk about experiments, and those experiments do support what the author claimed in the first paragraph.*
(B) To introduce a hypothesis about insect behavior	*The passage does introduce such a hypothesis, but it does so in the first paragraph, not the second one. This is the overall point of the passage, but the question asks about only the second paragraph. (True but not right)*
(C) To illustrate the ways in which grasshoppers are unsuitable for the wasp's purposes	*The passage doesn't say that the grasshoppers are unsuitable. This trap might be set for someone who is reading very superficially and draws an erroneous conclusion about the experiments with grasshoppers. (Out of scope)*
(D) To explore the significance of the wasp's varied reactions to certain stimuli	*The Point of the passage is that the wasp does not change her behavior even when the circumstances of her situation change. (Direct contradiction)*
(E) To acknowledge experimental evidence that does not support the author's thesis	*The evidence in the second paragraph does support the author's thesis. (Direct contradiction)*

All of the traps here were discussed earlier in the chapter; for a refresher, look at the primary purpose explanation on pages 60–61.

If a question asks about the entire passage, then you have a primary purpose question. Remind yourself of the overall point, using your map as needed.

If the question asks specifically about one paragraph in the context of the whole, then use your map to remind yourself what that one paragraph is about and how it fits into the overall story of the passage.

Try to come up with your own answer to the question before you look at the answers. Then, dive into those answers and start eliminating. Do check all five answers, even after you think you've found the right one. Finally, verify that your final answer matches both the question asked and the answer you articulated to yourself up front.

Don't forget to keep an eye out for the common traps (summarized in your Cheat Sheet on the next page).

Cheat Sheet

Primary Purpose Cheat Sheet

Identify
the Question

Primary Purpose:	The primary purpose (or function) of the passage is to …
	The author of the passage is primarily concerned with …
	Which of the following most accurately states the purpose of the passage?
	Which of the following titles best summarizes the passage?
	With which of the following would the author be most likely to agree?
Paragraph:	What is the purpose of the second paragraph?
	Which of the following best describes the relationship of the third paragraph to the passage as a whole?

4

Find the
Support

Use map or overall understanding of the passage.

Predict
an Answer

Articulate the point or the purpose of the paragraph *before* looking at the answer choices.

Eliminate

Check all of the answers! Common traps:

Trap	Characteristics
Direct contradiction	The passage says the opposite
Extreme	Extreme word *without support* in the passage
One word off	Looks very tempting but one or two words are wrong
Out of scope	Goes beyond what the passage says
True but not right	The passage does say this, but it does not answer the question asked

Photocopy this page for future review. Better yet, use this page as a guide to create your own review sheet—you'll remember the material better if you write it down yourself.

Problem Set

The three passages in this problem set appear in both Chapters 4 and 5, but different questions are presented in each chapter. You'll have a chance to try answering mixed sets of general and specific questions in Chapter 6.

Give yourself 2–3 minutes to read each passage and up to 60 seconds to answer each question. After you're done, review your point and passage map before you check the solutions, thinking about ways to improve your process next time. Then, check your work against the solution key.

Passage I: Japanese Swords

Historians have long recognized the Japanese sword, or *nihonto*, as one of the finest cutting weapons ever produced. But to regard the sword that is synonymous with (5) the samurai as merely a weapon is to ignore what makes it so special. The Japanese sword has always been considered a splendid weapon and even a spiritual entity. The traditional Japanese adage "the sword is the (10) soul of the samurai" reflects not only the sword's importance to its wielder but also its permanent connection to its creator, the master smith.

Master smiths may not have been con- (15) sidered artists in the classical sense, but each smith exerted great care in the process of creating swords, no two of which were ever forged in exactly the same way. Over hundreds of hours, two types of steel were (20) repeatedly heated, hammered and folded together into thousands of very thin layers, producing a sword with an extremely sharp and durable cutting edge and a flexible, shock-absorbing blade. It was (25) common, though optional, for a master smith to place a physical signature on a blade; moreover, each smith's secret forging techniques left an idiosyncratic structural signature on his blades. Each (30) master smith brought a high level of devotion, skill, and attention to detail to the sword-making process, and the sword itself was a reflection of his personal honor and ability. This effort made each blade (35) as distinctive as the samurai who wielded it, such that today the Japanese sword is recognized as much for its artistic merit as for its historical significance.

1. The primary purpose of the passage is to

  (A) challenge the observation that the Japanese sword is highly admired by historians

  (B) introduce new information about the forging of Japanese swords

  (C) discuss an obsolete weapon of great historical significance

  (D) argue that Japanese sword makers were motivated by honor

  (E) explain the value attributed to the Japanese sword

2. Which of the following is the primary function of the second paragraph?

  (A) To present an explanation for a change in perception

  (B) To determine the historical significance of Japanese swords

  (C) To discuss the artistic aspects associated with creating Japanese swords

  (D) To compare Japanese master smiths to classical artists

  (E) To review the complete process of making a Japanese sword

4

Passage J: Polygamy

Polygamy in Africa has been a popular topic for social research over the past half-century; it has been analyzed by many distinguished minds and in various well-publicized works.
(5) In 1961, when Remi Clignet published his book *Many Wives, Many Powers*, he was not alone in his view that in Africa co-wives may be perceived as direct and indirect sources of increased income and prestige.

(10)   By the 1970s, such arguments had become crystallized and popular. Many other African scholars who wrote on the subject became the new champions of this philosophy. For example, in 1983, John Mbiti pro-
(15) claimed that polygamy is an accepted and respectable institution serving many useful social purposes. Similarly, G.K. Nukunya, in his paper "Polygamy as a Symbol of Status," reiterated Mbiti's idea that a plurality of wives
(20) is a legitimate sign of affluence and power in the African society.

     The colonial missionary voice, however, provided consistent opposition to polygamy. Invoking the authority of the Bible, mission-
(25) aries argued that the practice was unethical and destructive of family life, and they propagated the view that Africans had to be coerced into abiding by the monogamous view of marriage favored by West-
(30) ern culture. In some instances, missionaries even dictated immediate divorce for newly-converted men who had already entered into polygamous marriages. Unfortunately, neither the missionary
(35) voice nor the scholarly voice considered the views of African women important. Although there was some awareness that women regarded polygamy as both a curse and a blessing, the distanced, albeit
(40) scientific, perspective of an outside observer predominated both at the pulpit and in scholarly writings.

     Contemporary research in the social sciences has begun to focus on
(45) the protagonist's voice in the study of culture, recognizing that the views and experiences of those who take part in a given reality ought to receive close examination. This privileging of
(50) the protagonist seems appropriate, particularly given that women in Africa have often used literary productions to comment on marriage, family, and gender relations.

1. **Which of the following best describes the primary purpose of the passage?**

    (A) To discuss scholarly works that view polygamy as a sign of prestige, respect, and affluence in the African society

    (B) To trace the origins of the missionary opposition to African polygamy

    (C) To argue for imposing restrictions on polygamy in African society

    (D) To explore the reasons for women's acceptance of polygamy

    (E) To discuss multiple perspectives on African polygamy and contrast them with contemporary research

2. **The third paragraph of the passage plays which of the following roles?**

    (A) It discusses the rationale for viewing polygamy as an indication of prestige and affluence in African society.

    (B) It supports the author's view that polygamy is unethical and destructive of family life.

    (C) It contrasts the views of the colonial missionaries with the position of the most recent contemporary research.

    (D) It describes the views on polygamy held by the colonial missionaries and indicates a flaw in this vision.

    (E) It demonstrates that the colonial missionaries were ignorant of the scholarly research on polygamy.

4

Passage K: Sweet Spot

Most tennis players strive to strike the ball on the racket's vibration node, more commonly known as the "sweet spot." However, many players are unaware of

(5) the existence of a second, lesser-known location on the racket face—the center of percussion—that will also greatly diminish the strain on a player's arm when the ball is struck.

(10)   In order to understand the physics of this second sweet spot, it is helpful to consider what would happen to a tennis racket if the player's hand were to vanish at the moment of impact with the ball. The impact of

(15) the ball would cause the racket to bounce backwards, resulting in a translational motion away from the ball. The tendency of this motion would be to jerk all parts of the racket, including the end of its handle, backward,

(20) or away from the ball. Unless the ball happened to hit precisely at the racket's center of mass, the racket would additionally experience a rotational motion around its center of mass—much as a penny that has been struck

(25) near its edge will start to spin. Whenever the ball hits the racket face, the effect of this rotational motion is to jerk the end of the handle forward, towards the ball. Depending on where the ball strikes the racket face,

(30) one or the other of these motions will predominate.

However, there is one point of impact, known as the center of percussion, which causes neither motion to

(35) predominate; if a ball strikes this point, the impact does not impart any motion to the end of the handle. The reason for this lack of motion is that the force on the upper part of the hand would be

(40) equal and opposite to the force on the lower part of the hand, resulting in no net force on the tennis player's hand or forearm. The center of percussion constitutes a second sweet spot because

(45) a tennis player's wrist is typically placed next to the end of the racket's handle. When the player strikes the ball at the center of percussion, her wrist is jerked neither forward nor backward, and she

(50) experiences greatly reduced vibration in the arm.

The manner in which a tennis player can detect the center of percussion on a given tennis racket follows from the

(55) nature of this second sweet spot. The center of percussion can be located via simple trial and error by holding the end of a tennis racket between the finger and thumb and throwing a ball onto the

(60) strings. If the handle jumps out of the player's hand, then the ball has missed the center of percussion.

1. **What is the primary message the author is trying to convey?**

   (A) A proposal for an improvement to the design of tennis rackets

   (B) An examination of the differences between the two types of sweet spot

   (C) A definition of the translational and rotational forces acting on a tennis racket

   (D) A description of the ideal area in which to strike every ball

   (E) An explanation of a lesser-known area on a tennis racket that reduces unwanted vibration

2. **What is the primary function served by paragraph two in the context of the entire passage?**

   (A) To establish the main idea of the passage

   (B) To provide an explanation of the mechanics of the phenomenon discussed in the passage

   (C) To introduce a counterargument that elucidates the main idea of the passage

   (D) To explain the physics of tennis

   (E) To explain why the main idea of the passage would be useful for tennis players

4

Solutions

The solutions show a sample passage map and the point, as well as explanations for each answer choice. Where appropriate, wrong answers have been labeled by wrong answer category.

Passage I: Japanese Swords

Historians have long recognized the Japanese sword, or *nihonto*, as one of the finest cutting weapons ever produced. But to regard the sword that is synonymous with
(5) the samurai as merely a weapon is to ignore what makes it so special. The Japanese sword has always been considered a splendid weapon and even a spiritual entity. The traditional Japanese adage "the sword is the
(10) soul of the samurai" reflects not only the sword's importance to its wielder but also its permanent connection to its creator, the master smith.

Master smiths may not have been con-
(15) sidered artists in the classical sense, but each smith exerted great care in the process of creating swords, no two of which were ever forged in exactly the same way. Over hundreds of hours, two types of steel were
(20) repeatedly heated, hammered and folded together into thousands of very thin layers, producing a sword with an extremely sharp and durable cutting edge and a flexible, shock-absorbing blade. It was
(25) common, though optional, for a master smith to place a physical signature on a blade; moreover, each smith's secret forging techniques left an idiosyncratic structural signature on his blades. Each
(30) master smith brought a high level of devotion, skill, and attention to detail to the sword-making process, and the sword itself was a reflection of his personal honor and ability. This effort made each blade
(35) as distinctive as the samurai who wielded it such that today the Japanese sword is recognized as much for its artistic merit as for its historical significance.

Sample passage map (yours will likely differ):

(1) *J sword: not just weapon, spirit*

(2) *Master smith: skilled*
       how to make
       sword: artistic merit, histor signif

The point (articulate to yourself): Japanese sword is a weapon *and* a work of art, important to both samurai and smith. The smiths were almost like artists.

1. The primary purpose of the passage is to

   (A) challenge the observation that the Japanese sword is highly admired by historians

   (B) introduce new information about the forging of Japanese swords

   (C) discuss an obsolete weapon of great historical significance

   (D) argue that Japanese sword makers were motivated by honor

   (E) explain the value attributed to the Japanese sword

The wording here indicates that this is a primary purpose question. Glance at your map and remind yourself of the point before you go to the answers.

(A) The passage does not challenge the idea that historians admired the swords; the entire passage reflects great admiration for the swords and their makers. (Direct contradiction)

(B) The second paragraph does talk about how swords are forged, but does not present this information as *new*. Moreover, information about the forging process is only one part of the passage; it is not the overall Point of the passage. (One word off)

(C) An *obsolete* weapon would no longer exist today; the passage does not indicate that Japanese swords are no longer used or no longer produced. (One word off)

(D) The passage does indicate that the swords were a reflection of the master smith's personal honor, but this is a narrow detail; it is not the point of the entire passage. (True but not right)

(E) CORRECT. The passage does explain the value of the sword to the samurai (in the first paragraph—*the sword is the soul of the samurai* [lines 9–10]) and to the master smith (in the second paragraph).

2. Which of the following is the primary function of the second paragraph?

(A) To present an explanation for a change in perception

(B) To determine the historical significance of Japanese swords

(C) To discuss the artistic aspects associated with creating Japanese swords

(D) To compare Japanese master smiths to classical artists

(E) To review the complete process of making a Japanese sword

This is a paragraph question. Glance at your map and articulate the purpose of the second paragraph to yourself before you check the answers.

The second paragraph mentions that smiths weren't artists in the classical sense but concludes by talking about the artistic merit of the sword. The description of the forging process emphasizes the depth of expertise and care with which the smith made the sword; the smith sometimes even signed it!

(A) The passage does not indicate that a general change in perception has occurred. Rather, the author is putting forth his own idea that smiths might be considered artists. (Out of scope)

(B) The last sentence of the paragraph does mention the historical significance, but the rest of the paragraph focuses on the forging process and the *artistic merit*. The paragraph does not actually discuss the historical significance. (Out of scope)

(C) CORRECT. The paragraph begins by indicating that the smiths *may not have been considered artists in the classical sense* (lines 14–15), but goes on to underscore the uniqueness of the finished products (no two were forged the same way, the swords were often signed, the finished product was not just a product but a reflection of the smith's personal honor and ability). The last sentence indicates that the swords are highly regarded for their *artistic merit* (line 37).

(D) While the passage does imply that the smiths might be considered artists, there is no mention of actual classical artists, nor is any comparison made. (Out of scope)

(E) The passage does provide some details of the sword-making process, but it does not review the *complete* process. (Extreme)

Passage J: Polygamy

Polygamy in Africa has been a popular topic for social research over the past half-century; it has been analyzed by many distinguished minds and in various well-publicized works.

(5) In 1961, when Remi Clignet published his book *Many Wives, Many Powers*, he was not alone in his view that in Africa co-wives may be perceived as direct and indirect sources of increased income and prestige.

(10) By the 1970s, such arguments had become crystallized and popular. Many other African scholars who wrote on the subject became the new champions of this philosophy. For example, in 1983, John Mbiti pro-

(15) claimed that polygamy is an accepted and respectable institution serving many useful social purposes. Similarly, G.K. Nukunya, in his paper "Polygamy as a Symbol of Status," reiterated Mbiti's idea that a plurality of wives

(20) is a legitimate sign of affluence and power in the African society.

The colonial missionary voice, however, provided consistent opposition to polygamy. Invoking the authority of the Bible, mission-

(25) aries argued that the practice was unethical and destructive of family life, and they propagated the view that Africans had to be coerced into abiding by the monoga-mous view of marriage favored by West-

(30) ern culture. In some instances, missionaries even dictated immediate divorce for newly-converted men who had already entered into polygamous marriages. Unfortunately, neither the missionary

(35) voice nor the scholarly voice considered the views of African women important. Although there was some awareness that women regarded polygamy as both a curse and a blessing, the distanced, albeit

(40) scientific, perspective of an outside observer predominated both at the pulpit and in scholarly writings.

Contemporary research in the social sciences has begun to focus on

(45) the protagonist's voice in the study of culture, recognizing that the views and experiences of those who take part in a given reality ought to receive close examination. This privileging of the pro-

(50) tagonist seems appropriate, particularly given that women in Africa have often used literary productions to comment on marriage, family, and gender relations.

Sample passage map (yours will likely differ):

① *Polyg Afr*
       '61 Clignet: P = income, prestige
② *70s, 80s: positive dtls*
③ *Missionary: against*
    neither listened to women
④ *Now: listening to women*

The point (articulate to yourself): Early scholars thought polygamy was a good thing. Missionaries were against it. Now, people are actually paying attention to what the women think.

1. Which of the following best describes the primary purpose of the passage?

  (A) To discuss scholarly works that view polygamy as a sign of prestige, respect, and afflu-
      ence in the African society

  (B) To trace the origins of the missionary opposition to African polygamy

  (C) To argue for imposing restrictions on polygamy in African society

  (D) To explore the reasons for women's acceptance of polygamy

  (E) To discuss multiple perspectives on African polygamy and contrast them with contem-
      porary research

This is a primary purpose question. Glance at your map and remind yourself of the point before you go to the answers.

(A) The first two paragraphs do talk about works that portray polygamy positively, but the rest of the passage explores different viewpoints. This is one detail, not the overall point. (True but not right)

(B) The passage does discuss missionary opposition to polygamy, but does not detail its origins. (Out of scope)

(C) While it might be possible that the author would support a restriction on polygamy, the passage itself does not make such an argument. In fact, the passage never directly supports a particular position on polygamy—rather, it explores different perspectives on the topic. (Out of scope)

(D) The passage does indicate that women found polygamy *a curse and a blessing* (lines 38–39), but it does not explore their reasons for thinking that polygamy can sometimes be a blessing. (Out of scope)

(E) CORRECT. The first few paragraphs look at different perspectives (scholars, missionaries). Then the passage ends by indicating that contemporary researchers are paying attention to what women think (something the earlier groups didn't do).

MANHATTAN
PREP

2. The third paragraph of the passage plays which of the following roles?

(A) It discusses the rationale for viewing polygamy as an indication of prestige and affluence in African society.

(B) It supports the author's view that polygamy is unethical and destructive of family life.

(C) It contrasts the views of the colonial missionaries with the position of the most recent contemporary research.

(D) It describes the views on polygamy held by the colonial missionaries and indicates a flaw in this vision.

(E) It demonstrates that the colonial missionaries were ignorant of the scholarly research on polygamy.

This is a paragraph question. Glance at your map and articulate the purpose of the third paragraph to yourself before you check the answers.

The third paragraph begins by discussing the missionary view of polygamy (against) and goes on to say that both the missionaries and the scholars mentioned earlier failed to take into account the point of view of the women involved in these polygamous marriages.

(A) This occurs in the first two paragraphs, not the third. (True but not right)

(B) The author does not present a personal viewpoint in the passage. (Out of scope)

(C) The third paragraph does discuss the missionary viewpoint, but contemporary research is discussed in the *fourth* paragraph, not the third. (True but not right)

(D) CORRECT. The paragraph does talk about the missionary view of polygamy. It also indicates a flaw in this thinking: the missionaries failed to consider the views of women in polygamous marriages.

(E) The passage presents the missionary view separately from the views of the scholars mentioned earlier in the passage; it does not indicate whether the missionaries were familiar with the scholarly position. (Out of scope)

MANHATTAN
PREP

Passage K: Sweet Spot

Most tennis players strive to strike the ball on the racket's vibration node, more commonly known as the "sweet spot." However, many players are unaware of
(5) the existence of a second, lesser-known location on the racket face—the center of percussion—that will also greatly diminish the strain on a player's arm when the ball is struck.
(10)   In order to understand the physics of this second sweet spot, it is helpful to consider what would happen to a tennis racket if the player's hand were to vanish at the moment of impact with the ball. The impact of
(15) the ball would cause the racket to bounce backwards, resulting in a translational motion away from the ball. The tendency of this motion would be to jerk all parts of the racket, including the end of its handle, backward,
(20) or away from the ball. Unless the ball happened to hit precisely at the racket's center of mass, the racket would additionally experience a rotational motion around its center of mass—much as a penny that has been struck
(25) near its edge will start to spin. Whenever the ball hits the racket face, the effect of this rotational motion is to jerk the end of the handle forward, towards the ball. Depending on where the ball strikes the racket face,
(30) one or the other of these motions will predominate.

However, there is one point of impact, known as the center of percussion, which causes neither motion to
(35) predominate; if a ball strikes this point, the impact does not impart any motion to the end of the handle. The reason for this lack of motion is that the force on the upper part of the hand would be
(40) equal and opposite to the force on the lower part of the hand, resulting in no net force on the tennis player's hand or forearm. The center of percussion constitutes a second sweet spot because
(45) a tennis player's wrist is typically placed next to the end of the racket's handle. When the player strikes the ball at the center of percussion, her wrist is jerked neither forward nor backward, and she
(50) experiences greatly reduced vibration in the arm.

The manner in which a tennis player can detect the center of percussion on a given tennis racket follows from the
(55) nature of this second sweet spot. The center of percussion can be located via simple trial and error by holding the end of a tennis racket between the finger and thumb and throwing a ball onto the
(60) strings. If the handle jumps out of the player's hand, then the ball has missed the center of percussion.

4

Sample passage map (yours will likely differ):

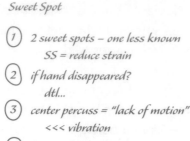

Sweet Spot

① *2 sweet spots – one less known*
    SS = reduce strain
② *if hand disappeared?*
    dtl...
③ *center percuss = "lack of motion"*
    <<< vibration
④ *how to find center percuss*

The point (articulate to yourself): People know about one sweet spot but not the other. Both reduce vibration in the arm. (Plus lots of technical details—ignore for now!)

1. What is the primary message the author is trying to convey?

(A) A proposal for an improvement to the design of tennis rackets

(B) An examination of the differences between the two types of sweet spot

(C) A definition of the translational and rotational forces acting on a tennis racket

(D) A description of the ideal area in which to strike every ball

(E) An explanation of a lesser-known area on a tennis racket that reduces unwanted vibration

The words *primary message* indicate that this is a primary purpose question. Glance at your map and remind yourself of the point before you go to the answers.

(A) The passage doesn't talk about this at all. (Out of scope)

(B) It does talk about two different types of sweet spot. Leave this in for now.

(C) One paragraph did mention these forces, but that was only one paragraph. This is not the point of the whole thing. (True but not right)

(D) The passage does say that striking the ball at a sweet spot can reduce vibration, but it never says that spot is the ideal area in which to strike *every* ball. (Extreme)

(E) It does talk about this. Leave this in.

Compare answers (B) and (E) to the support in the passage. The first paragraph mentions both sweet spots. After that, though, the passage focuses just on the lesser-known one; it doesn't go back-and-forth contrasting the two. Answer (E) is more appropriate than answer (B).

The correct answer is **(E)**.

MANHATTAN
PREP

2. What is the primary function served by paragraph two in the context of the entire passage?

   (A) To establish the main idea of the passage

   (B) To provide an explanation of the mechanics of the phenomenon discussed in the passage

   (C) To introduce a counterargument that elucidates the main idea of the passage

   (D) To explain the physics of tennis

   (E) To explain why the main idea of the passage would be useful for tennis players

This is a paragraph question. Glance at your map and articulate the purpose of the second paragraph to yourself before you check the answers.

The opening sentence of the second paragraph talks about the physics of the second sweet spot and then goes into lots of detail about what would happen if the player's hand vanished and various forces and … wait! Don't get sucked into the detail. The first sentence is probably enough. Check the answers.

   (A) The first paragraph establishes the main idea. The second paragraph talks about the physics of hitting a tennis ball. (Out of scope)

   (B) CORRECT. The second paragraph does explain the physics, or the *mechanics*, of the phenomenon mentioned in the first paragraph.

   (C) The second paragraph does elucidate the main idea, but it is not a counterargument to anything. (One word off)

   (D) The paragraph does discuss the physical forces relevant to the sweet spot, but it does not explain all of the physics behind the game of tennis. That would be a very long passage! (Out of scope)

   (E) The first and third paragraphs explain why the main idea is useful: to reduce vibration in the arm. The second paragraph does not do this. (True but not right)

4

Chapter 5

Reading Comprehension

Specific Questions

In This Chapter...

Chapter 5
Specific Questions

Most of the questions you receive on the GMAT will ask you about specific details in the passage. On average, expect to spend 60–90 seconds on each specific question.

There are three primary types of specific questions:

1. **Detail questions.** These questions ask you to find a specific detail explicitly stated in the passage.

2. **Inference questions.** The answer will *not* be stated explicitly in the passage, but the correct answer can be proven to be true using information stated in the passage.

3. **Specific Purpose questions.** These questions ask you *why* the author mentions a specific piece of information or employs a particular example.

You may also see the occasional rare question type, such as a strengthen or weaken question. While these don't show up often on Reading Comprehension, when they do, you can use your Critical Reasoning strategies for strengthen or weaken questions.

Four Steps to the Answer

You'll use the same process you learned for general questions in Chapter 4 in order to answer specific questions:

Step 1: Identify the question. This chapter will tell you the common language to expect for the different question types.

Step 2: Find the support. Specific questions will require you to go back into the passage. Use your map to quickly figure out where to go, then read the relevant one to three sentences. Do not skip this step! Many specific questions have trap answers designed specifically to catch people who don't look for support in the passage.

Step 3: Predict an answer. Take a look at the question again and, using the relevant passage text, try to formulate a rough answer in your own words. But there's a caveat: this won't work 100% of the time. This chapter will explain what to do when you can't predict the answer.

Step 4: Eliminate and find a match. Evaluate each answer, while keeping in mind your predicted answer. When you find a potential match, leave it in and continue to eliminate.

- If you eliminate four answers, great! Pick the remaining one and move on.

- If you still have two or three answers left, compare the answers to the relevant information in the passage. If the answers are very similar, you may also compare them to each other.

- If you still have four or five answers left, make sure you are answering the right question! After that, it's probably best to cut your losses: guess and move on.

Practice Passage: Electroconvulsive Therapy

Give yourself approximately eight minutes to read the passage below and answer the questions that follow.

Electroconvulsive therapy (ECT) is a controversial psychiatric treatment involving the induction of a seizure in a patient by passing electricity through the brain. While beneficial
(5) effects of electrically induced seizures are evident and predictable in most patients, a unified mechanism of action has not yet been established and remains the subject of numerous investigations. ECT is extremely
(10) effective against severe depression, some acute psychotic states, and mania, though, like many medical procedures, it has its risks.

Since the inception of ECT in 1938, the public has held a strongly negative con-
(15) ception of the procedure. Initially, doctors employed unmodified ECT. Patients were rendered instantly unconscious by the electrical current, but the strength of the muscle contractions from uncontrolled motor
(20) seizures often led to compression fractures of the spine or damage to the teeth. In addition to the effect this physical trauma had on public sentiment, graphic examples of abuse documented in books and movies, such as
(25) Ken Kesey's *One Flew Over the Cuckoo's Nest*, portrayed ECT as punitive, cruel, overused, and violative of patients' legal rights.

Modern ECT is virtually unrecognizable from its earlier days. The treatment is modified
(30) by the muscle relaxant succinylcholine, which renders muscle contractions practically nonexistent. Additionally, patients are given a general anesthetic. Thus, the patient is asleep and fully unaware during the
(35) procedure, and the only outward sign of a seizure may be the rhythmic movement of the patient's hand or foot. ECT is generally used in severely depressed patients for whom psychotherapy and medication
(40) prove ineffective. It may also be considered when there is an imminent risk of suicide, since antidepressants often take several weeks to work effectively. Exactly how ECT exerts its effects is not known,
(45) but repeated applications affect several neurotransmitters in the brain, including serotonin, norepinephrine, and dopamine.

ECT has proven effective, but it is not without controversy. Though decades-
(50) old studies showing brain cell death have been refuted in recent research, many patients do report loss of memory for events that occurred in the days, weeks, or months surrounding the ECT. Some
(55) patients have also reported that their short-term memories continue to be affected for months after ECT, though some doctors argue that this memory malfunction may reflect the type of amnesia that
(60) sometimes results from severe depression.

1. **According to the passage, why has ECT been viewed negatively by the public?**

   (A) Though ECT is effective in many cases, the medical community is not certain exactly how it works.

   (B) Cultural depictions of ECT implied that the therapy infringed upon the lawful rights of those receiving the treatment.

   (C) Effective use of ECT requires exposure to concerning medications, such as muscle relaxants and anesthesia.

   (D) ECT does not benefit individuals with anxiety disorders.

   (E) ECT cannot be performed without subsequent loss of memory in the patient.

2. **Which of the following can be inferred about the way in which the modern form of ECT works?**

   (A) Greater amounts of the neurotransmitters serotonin, norepinephrine, and dopamine seem to reduce symptoms of depression.

   (B) ECT cannot be used prior to attempting psychotherapy or medication.

   (C) Succinylcholine completely immobilizes the patient's body.

   (D) ECT generally works faster than antidepressants.

   (E) One ECT treatment is often sufficient to reduce symptoms of depression significantly.

3. **The author mentions amnesia as a possible side effect of severe depression in order to**

   (A) acknowledge one of the possible negative side effects associated with ECT

   (B) emphasize the seriousness of severe depression as a debilitating disease

   (C) introduce a possible alternative cause for short-term memory loss reported by some patients

   (D) draw a connection between brain cell death and short-term memory loss

   (E) refute claims that ECT is responsible for any form of amnesia in patients

4. **Each of the following is cited in the passage as a current or historical criticism of electroconvulsive therapy EXCEPT**

   (A) ECT may cause the death of brain cells and memory loss

   (B) in certain cases, ECT was portrayed as a means to punish individuals

   (C) ECT had the potential to be used in inappropriate situations

   (D) early forms of ECT did not adequately protect patients from secondary harm brought on by the treatment

   (E) repeated applications of ECT affect several neurotransmitters in the brain

5

The questions above fall into four distinct question types. The sections below will each cover one type and provide an explanation of the relevant question. First, here's what a reader might be thinking while reading the passage and jotting down a map:

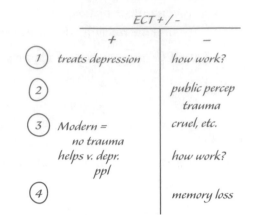

ECT (electricity → seizure) has positives and negatives. Don't know how it works, but it is effective against depression and some other things.

Public doesn't like ECT. Early forms caused serious bodily trauma. Books and movies showed that it was cruel, infringed on rights, etc.

Modern ECT is much better. No trauma. Still don't know how it works but it helps really depressed people who can't get help in other ways.

It still has drawbacks, though, primarily around memory loss.

Here's a simple story for the passage:

> *ECT was pretty bad at first but it's better now. They don't really know how it works, but it does work for depression. Even though ECT is better now, it still has some drawbacks.*

Detail Questions

Detail questions almost always include the language "according to the passage." If you see this language, then you are being asked to find a particular piece of information, explicitly stated in the passage, that answers that particular question.

Many times, the question will give you enough information to find the specific answer in the passage before you look at the answers. Where does the question stem below signal that you should look?

> 1. According to the passage, why has ECT been viewed negatively by the public?

The question stem specifically references the public's negative view of ECT. This concept is the topic sentence of the second paragraph, so your passage map should contain some reference to this idea.

Return to paragraph 2 and try to formulate your own answer before you dive into the answer choices:

> Since the inception of ECT in 1938, the public has held a strongly negative conception of the procedure. Initially, doctors employed unmodified ECT. Patients were rendered instantly unconscious by the electrical current, but the strength of the muscle contractions from uncontrolled motor seizures often led to compression fractures of the spine or damage to the teeth. In addition to the effect this physical trauma had on public sentiment, graphic examples of abuse documented in books and movies, such as Ken Kesey's *One Flew Over the Cuckoo's Nest*, portrayed ECT as punitive, cruel, overused, and violative of patients' legal rights (lines 13–27).

The first part of the paragraph discusses certain types of physical trauma (spinal fractures, damage to the teeth). The second part talks about graphic examples of abuse portrayed in books and movies. The correct answer should address one or both of those two topics.

Time to eliminate! Try to identify any trap answer types that you have already learned.

(A) Though ECT is effective in many cases, the medical community is not certain exactly how it works.

The passage states both that ECT can be effective and that the exact mechanism by which it works is unknown. Neither of these, however, is cited by the passage as a reason that the public has viewed ECT negatively. (True but not right)

(B) Cultural depictions of ECT implied that the therapy infringed upon the lawful rights of those receiving the treatment.

CORRECT. *The last sentence of the second paragraph says that examples…documented in books and movies…portrayed ECT as…violative of patient's legal rights (lines 23–27).*

(C) Effective use of ECT requires exposure to concerning medications, such as muscle relaxants and anesthesia.

The passage does state that ECT now uses muscle relaxants and anesthesia, but the passage does not call these medications concerning. *If anything, the passage considers these positive advances, as* the patient is asleep and fully unaware *(lines 33–34). (One word off)*

(D) ECT does not benefit individuals with anxiety disorders.

The passage does not mention individuals with anxiety disorders. (Out of scope)

(E) ECT cannot be performed without subsequent loss of memory in the patient.

The last paragraph does mention that ECT can result in memory loss, but does not say that this side effect is always present. (Nor does the passage mention public conception with respect to memory loss.) (Extreme)

The wrong answers represent several common traps, all of which were first presented in Chapter 4, General Questions. For a quick review, reference your Cheat Sheet at the end of Chapter 4 (page 63).

If you see a question that begins *According to the passage …*, you know you have a detail question. Use your map to figure out what paragraph you'll need; in this case, the word *public* was a good clue to look in paragraph 2.

Try to formulate an answer to the question before you look at the answer choices. Note that there may be more than one possibility. In this case, the correct answer could have talked about the bodily trauma or about the depictions in books and movies.

At times, you may struggle to understand certain parts of a passage, in which case you may not be able to predict an answer. In this case, remind yourself of the main points in any relevant paragraph(s) and then try to test the answers against those main points. If this doesn't help, guess and move on.

Inference Questions

Inference questions ask you to find an answer that must be true based on information presented in the passage—but the information in the answer choice will *not* be explicitly presented in the passage.

For example, if your boss tells you that Acme Co is your company's most important client, what can you infer?

You might imagine that Acme Co is responsible for a larger chunk of the company's revenue than is any other client. This might be a reasonable inference in the real world, but it will lead you to a wrong answer on the GMAT. Why? Because it doesn't *have* to be true.

The GMAT is not asking you to come up with reasonable real-world inferences. Instead, it is asking you to deduce what must be true given the available evidence.

If Acme Co is the company's most important client, what else has to be true?

For starters, your company has to have at least one other client. If Acme Co were the only client, then your boss couldn't call it the most important client.

If one of the company's other clients is Widget Inc, you could also correctly infer that Widget Inc is not the company's most important client—that spot is already taken!

Notice that you have no idea *why* Acme Co is the most important client. GMAT answers that make this kind of move are often tempting, but they are incorrect. The boss just stated a fact and didn't give you any insight into the reason for that fact.

Which problem in the Electroconvulsive Therapy set was the inference problem? The wording of the question stem will tell you:

> 2. Which of the following can be inferred about the way in which the modern form of ECT works?

In this case, the word *inferred* is in the question stem. Any form of the words *infer*, *imply*, or *suggest* indicates that you have an inference question.

Modern ECT is first mentioned in the third paragraph, so look there to find your support. Step 3 (predict an answer), however, is pretty tough: the paragraph is all about how ECT works. In this case, it would be tough for anyone to try to predict an answer in advance.

Instead, return to the third paragraph to remind yourself of the type of information it contains, then start to check the answers, crossing off anything you cannot prove to be true based on information from that paragraph.

> Modern ECT is virtually unrecognizable from its earlier days. The treatment is modified by the muscle relaxant succinylcholine, which renders muscle contractions practically non-existent. Additionally, patients are given a general anesthetic. Thus, the patient is asleep and fully unaware during the procedure, and the only outward sign of a seizure may be the rhythmic movement of the patient's hand or foot. ECT is generally used in severely depressed patients for whom psychotherapy and medication prove ineffective. It may also be considered when there is an imminent risk of suicide, since antidepressants often take several weeks to work effectively. Exactly how ECT exerts its effects is not known, but repeated applications affect several neurotransmitters in the brain, including serotonin, norepinephrine, and dopamine (lines 28–47).

The modern form of ECT is much safer for patients and very effective in certain cases. Move to the answers and check them against the paragraph. Fortunately, it should be possible to identify some familiar traps on this new question type.

(A) Greater amounts of the neurotransmitters serotonin, norepinephrine, and dopamine seem to reduce symptoms of depression.

The third paragraph does talk about these neurotransmitters. Some people might think this is plausible in the real world, but be careful—you have to find proof in the passage. The third paragraph says only that repeated applications (line 45) *of ECT affect these neurotransmitters. It does not indicate what effect these neurotransmitters have on depression. (Out of scope)*

(B) ECT cannot be used prior to attempting psychotherapy or medication.

Whenever you see an extreme word, check whether the passage justifies the usage. In this case, the third paragraph does not justify the use of the word cannot; *it implies only that those other therapies are tried first at least some of the time. (Extreme)*

(C) Succinylcholine completely immobilizes the patient's body.

The third paragraph states that succinylcholine renders muscle contractions practically nonexistent (lines 31–32). *The qualifier* practically *means the muscle contractions are almost gone, but not entirely. The word* completely, *then, is too extreme. (Extreme)*

(D) ECT generally works faster than antidepressants.

CORRECT. *The third paragraph states that ECT* may also be considered when there is an imminent risk of suicide, since antidepressants often take several weeks to work effectively *(lines 40–43). If ECT is used when there is an* imminent, *or* immediate, *risk, because antidepressants take a while to work, then ECT must generally work more quickly than antidepressants.*

(E) One ECT treatment is often sufficient to reduce symptoms of depression significantly.

The passage does not mention the number of treatments necessary to reduce symptoms significantly. At one point, it does mention repeated applications (line 45) *so, if anything, it appears that more than one treatment might be typical. (Out of scope)*

5

If you see a question that contains some form of the words *infer, imply,* or *suggest,* then you know you have an inference question. In most cases, the question stem will also contain some specific info that will help you to determine which paragraph you'll need. In this case, a key term in the question stem is mentioned for the first time at the beginning of the third paragraph.

If you can, try to formulate an answer to the question before you look at the answer choices. Note that, sometimes, the question stem will be too vague to predict a solid answer in advance (this can happen on both detail and inference questions). When this happens (or when you don't understand the information well enough to come up with your own predicting answer), remind yourself of the main points in any relevant paragraph(s) or sentences and then start to test the answers.

If you find yourself struggling with inference questions, you may want to consider cross-training in Critical Reasoning. This same skill is tested in inference CR questions, and you will find that it is a crucial element of your success on the Verbal section. On either question type, it can be helpful to review your work by comparing each answer choice carefully to the supporting text. This will help you learn to distinguish a valid inference from an answer choice that goes too far.

Specific Purpose Questions

Specific purpose questions are not quite as common as either detail or inference questions, but you can expect to see at least one or two in the Verbal section. These questions ask you for what purpose, or *why*, the author mentions a specific piece of information.

As with inference questions, you can't just repeat back what the passage explicitly states. Instead, you have to do a little bit of processing. For instance, consider this information:

> Silicon chip manufacturers struggle to maintain profit margins due to the exorbitantly high overhead costs associated with building semiconductor factories. Such factories typically cost a minimum of two billion dollars to build and may be obsolete within three to five years. As such, the manufacturers seek out customers who need very high volumes of products, allowing the overhead costs to be spread out over a large number of units.

Here's the question stem:

> The author states that semiconductor factories may become obsolete within three to five years of being built in order to

Why does the author talk about this particular detail? In the prior sentence, the author asserts that these factories have *exorbitantly high overhead costs*, so she is providing information to support her contention that these costs really are very high. The correct answer might say something like:

> emphasize the high costs associated with manufacturing silicon chips

Here's the question from the ECT passage:

> 3. The author mentions amnesia as a possible side effect of severe depression in order to

What similarities can you spot between the semiconductor question stem and the one above? Both talk about the *author*. Both finish with *in order to*. Specific purpose questions are typically structured to say *the author* (mentions some specific detail) *in order to* … and then you have to fill in the blank with the answer that explains why the author mentioned that detail.

So, where did the author talk about amnesia and severe depression?

You may not have noted this very specific detail about amnesia in your map, so you may have to go on a hunt. The passage mentions *severe depression* in three out of the four paragraphs, so do a scan for the word *amnesia*. Also, amnesia is a type of memory loss. You might have noted or you may remember that the last paragraph talks about memory loss. Here's the relevant text from the fourth paragraph:

> Some patients have also reported that their short-term memories continue to be affected for months after ECT, though some doctors argue that this memory malfunction may reflect the type of amnesia that sometimes results from severe depression.

On to step 3: formulate your own answer to the question. *Why* does the author bring up amnesia in the context of severe depression?

Some people appear to attribute short-term memory problems to ECT; this is consistent with much of the rest of the passage, which discusses negative side effects and risks associated with ECT. The second half of the sentence, however, indicates that some think that these symptoms might actually be caused by the depression itself. In other words, it's possible that this particular side effect is not actually a result of ECT.

5

The author, then, is pointing out that not every possible negative effect is actually due to ECT. What answer choice goes along with this idea? (Also, try to identify any wrong answer traps that you have already learned.)

(A) acknowledge one of the possible negative side effects associated with ECT	*The passage does talk about many negative side effects associated with ECT, but the reference to amnesia is intended to introduce the idea that certain side effects actually might not be due to ECT. (Direct contradiction)*
(B) emphasize the seriousness of severe depression as a debilitating disease	*This choice sounds very tempting: in the real world, amnesia is a very serious issue and severe depression is a debilitating disease. However, depression is mentioned only as a possible alternative cause; the passage does not state that the amnesia is definitely a result of the depression. (True but not right)*
(C) introduce a possible alternative cause for short-term memory loss reported by some patients	**CORRECT.** *The first half of the sentence brings up patient reports of memory loss due to ECT; the second half indicates that some doctors think this memory loss might actually be due to amnesia from depression.*
(D) draw a connection between brain cell death and short-term memory loss	*The fourth paragraph mentions both brain cell death and short-term memory loss. The passage does not connect the two ideas, however. In fact, it says that reports of brain cell death have been refuted, though memory loss is still in evidence. (Mix-up)*
(E) refute claims that ECT is responsible for any form of amnesia in patients	*The sentence does offer a possible alternative cause, but ECT is not definitively ruled out as one possible cause. (Extreme)*

The wrong answers represent several common traps, one of which hasn't shown up in earlier problems. A **mix-up** is a tricky trap in which the test writers use wording straight from the passage to convey a different meaning than what is presented in the passage. They are expecting you to say, "That sounds familiar," and jump on the choice without giving it too much thought, and in fact that's exactly what many test-takers do. In answer (D) above, the key words used are all straight from the passage. The meaning of the answer, however, does not fit with the author's reason for mentioning amnesia. In fact, the answer does not even convey what the passage really said.

In order to is the most common clue that you have a specific purpose question; if the question says the author brought up some detail *in order to* do something, then you're trying to figure out why the author brought up that detail.

Use your map to figure out what paragraph you'll need; in this case, the words *amnesia* and *severe depression* indicated the fourth paragraph.

Whenever possible, try to formulate an answer to the question before you look at the answer choices. If you can't, remind yourself of the main points in any relevant sentences or paragraph(s) and then start to test the answers.

EXCEPT Questions

Any question type can also be written as an EXCEPT question; most of the time, when you see an EXCEPT question, you'll be dealing with a detail question or an inference question.

Here is the fourth question from the ECT passage. What question type is it?

> 4. Each of the following is cited in the passage as a current or historical criticism of electrocon-
>   vulsive therapy EXCEPT

The language *each of the following is cited* indicates that this is a detail question. The information in four of the answers is explicitly stated in the passage. The fifth answer, the one not cited in the passage, is the correct answer.

Follow the same process you would normally use for a detail question, with one twist.

It would be inefficient to try to find all of the criticisms of ECT in the passage first and only then go check the answers. Instead, go straight to the answers and use the keywords to try to find the information in the passage. If you've spent more than about 15–20 seconds on an answer and still haven't found it in the passage, leave it and move to the next answer.

As you work, label the answers either True or False on your scrap paper. True (or T) means that indeed, the answer is cited in the passage as a criticism of ECT. False means that it is not. You will cross off the four true answers and pick the odd one out, the lone false answer.

Also, note one important thing about the question: it asks for *current or historical criticism*, so something that was once criticized but is no longer considered problematic today would still count as a criticism of ECT.

(A) ECT may cause the death of brain cells and memory loss.	*True. The fourth paragraph mentions that very old research showed brain cell death (even though that research has been refuted today) and that memory loss is an ongoing concern.*
(B) In certain cases, ECT was portrayed as a means to punish individuals.	*True. Line 26 indicates that ECT was portrayed as punitive.*
(C) ECT had the potential to be used in inappropriate situations.	*True. Tricky! Line 26 indicates that ECT was portrayed as overused. If a treatment is overused, then at least some of those uses shouldn't be happening, or are inappropriate.*
(D) Early forms of ECT did not adequately protect patients from secondary harm brought on by the treatment.	*True. Lines 20–21 indicate that early forms of ECT often led to compression fractures of the spine or damage to the teeth.*
(E) Repeated applications of ECT affect several neurotransmitters in the brain.	**CORRECT.** *False. Lines 45–47 do mention that ECT affects neurotransmitters, but this information is not presented as a criticism of ECT. Rather, it is presented as a partial means of understanding how ECT works.*

The standard wrong answer trap categories don't apply to EXCEPT questions. The four wrong answers are "right" in the sense that they would be correct answers on a regular question. The one correct answer can fall into one of the standard trap categories. Which trap does answer (E), above, represent?

According to the passage, it is true that ECT affects neurotransmitters, but it is false that this was *cited in the passage as a current or historical criticism* of ECT. So Answer (E) is a variation of a true but not right trap answer.

EXCEPT questions are not a separate type of question; any of the main question types could be presented as an EXCEPT question. Use your usual clues to identify the question type. Then, reverse steps 2–4: go straight to the answers and try to find them in the passage. You're going to cross off the four true answers (for which you will find support in the passage) and select the one false answer.

Cheat Sheet

Specific Question Cheat Sheet

Identify the Question	**Detail:**	Most common: *According to the passage…*
		indicates explicitly …
		mentions (or *proposes*) *which of the following …*
	Inference:	Most common: *infer, imply, suggest provides support for …*
		author would be most likely to describe (or *predict*) X
	Specific Purpose:	Most common clue: *in order to*
		The author's reference (to X) *serves primarily to …*
	EXCEPT:	Any can also be EXCEPT questions. Use keywords from the answers to find the support in the passage.

Find the Support

Use your map to find specific paragraph or sentences needed. If you can't, go to answers to try to work backwards. If this doesn't work, guess and move on.

Predict an Answer

Try to formulate an answer in your own words. If you can't, go to answers to try to work backwards. If this doesn't work, guess and move on.

Eliminate

Check all of the answers! Common traps include the following.

Trap	Characteristics
Direct contradiction	The passage says the opposite.
Extreme	Extreme word *without support* in the passage.
One word off	Looks very tempting but one or two words are wrong.
Out of scope	Goes beyond what the passage says.
Mix-up	Uses words directly from the passage, but the meaning is not what the passage says.
True but not right	The passage says this (or it's true in the real world), but it does not answer the question asked.

Photocopy this page for future review. Better yet, use this page as a guide to create your own review sheet—you'll remember the material better if you write it down yourself.

Problem Set

The three passages in this problem set appear in both Chapters 4 and 5, but different questions are presented in each chapter. You'll have a chance to try answering mixed sets of general and specific questions in Chapter 6.

Give yourself 2–3 minutes to read each passage and another 60 seconds to answer each question. After you're done, review your point and passage map before you check the solutions to see whether you can think of any ways to improve your process next time. Then, check your work against the solution key.

Passage I: Japanese Swords

Historians have long recognized the Japanese sword, or *nihonto*, as one of the finest cutting weapons ever produced. But to regard the sword that is synonymous with
(5) the samurai as merely a weapon is to ignore what makes it so special. The Japanese sword has always been considered a splendid weapon and even a spiritual entity. The traditional Japanese adage "the sword is the
(10) soul of the samurai" reflects not only the sword's importance to its wielder but also its permanent connection to its creator, the master smith.

Master smiths may not have been con-
(15) sidered artists in the classical sense, but each smith exerted great care in the process of creating swords, no two of which were ever forged in exactly the same way. Over hundreds of hours, two types of steel were
(20) repeatedly heated, hammered and folded together into thousands of very thin layers, producing a sword with an extremely sharp and durable cutting edge and a flexible, shock-absorbing blade. It was
(25) common, though optional, for a master smith to place a physical signature on a blade; moreover, each smith's secret forging techniques left an idiosyncratic structural signature on his blades. Each
(30) master smith brought a high level of devotion, skill, and attention to detail to the sword-making process, and the sword itself was a reflection of his personal honor and ability. This effort made each blade
(35) as distinctive as the samurai who wielded it such that today the Japanese sword is recognized as much for its artistic merit as for its historical significance.

1. **Which of the following can be inferred about the structural signature of a Japanese sword?**

    (A) It is an inscription that the smith places on the blade during the forging process.

    (B) It refers to the particular characteristics of a blade created by a smith's unique forging process.

    (C) It suggests that each blade can be traced back to a known master smith.

    (D) It reflects the soul of the samurai who wielded the sword.

    (E) It refers to the actual curved shape of the blade.

2. **Each of the following is mentioned in the passage EXCEPT**

    (A) Every Japanese sword has a unique structure that can be traced back to a special forging process.

    (B) Master smiths kept their forging techniques secret.

    (C) The Japanese sword was considered by some to have a spiritual quality.

    (D) Master smiths are now considered artists by most major historians.

    (E) The Japanese sword is considered both a work of art and a historical artifact.

3. **The author explains the way in which swords were made in order to**

    (A) establish that the Japanese sword is the most important handheld weapon in history

    (B) claim that the skill of the samurai is what made each Japanese sword unique

    (C) support the contention that the master smiths might be considered artists as well as craftsmen

    (D) illustrate that master smiths were more concerned with the artistic merit of their blades than with the blades' practical qualities

    (E) demonstrate that the Japanese sword has more historical importance than artistic importance

5

Passage J: Polygamy

Polygamy in Africa has been a popular topic for social research over the past half-century; it has been analyzed by many distinguished minds and in various well-publicized works.

(5) In 1961, when Remi Clignet published his book *Many Wives, Many Powers*, he was not alone in his view that in Africa co-wives may be perceived as direct and indirect sources of increased income and prestige.

(10) By the 1970s, such arguments had become crystallized and popular. Many other African scholars who wrote on the subject became the new champions of this philosophy. For example, in 1983, John Mbiti pro-(15) claimed that polygamy is an accepted and respectable institution serving many useful social purposes. Similarly, G.K. Nukunya, in his paper "Polygamy as a Symbol of Status," reiterated Mbiti's idea that a plurality of (20) wives is a legitimate sign of affluence and power in the African society.

The colonial missionary voice, however, provided consistent opposition to polygamy. Invoking the authority of the (25) Bible, missionaries argued that the practice was unethical and destructive of family life, and they propagated the view that Africans had to be coerced into abiding by the monogamous view of marriage favored (30) by Western culture. In some instances, missionaries even dictated immediate divorce for newly-converted men who had already entered into polygamous marriages. Unfortunately, neither the (35) missionary voice nor the scholarly voice considered the views of African women important. Although there was some awareness that women regarded polygamy as both a curse and a blessing, (40) the distanced, albeit scientific, perspective of an outside observer predominated both at the pulpit and in scholarly writings.

Contemporary research in the so-(45) cial sciences has begun to focus on the protagonist's voice in the study of culture, recognizing that the views and experiences of those who take part in a given reality ought to receive close examination. (50) This privileging of the protagonist seems appropriate, particularly given that women in Africa have often used literary productions to comment on marriage, family, and gender relations.

5

1. According to the passage, colonial missionaries and popular scholars shared which of the following traits in their approach to the issue of polygamy?

(A) Both considered polygamy a sign of social status and success.

(B) Neither accounted for the views of local women.

(C) Both attempted to limit the prevalence of polygamy.

(D) Both pointed out polygamy's destructive effects on family life.

(E) Both exhibited a somewhat negative attitude towards polygamy.

2. The author implies which of the following about Nukunya and Mbiti's works?

(A) From their point of view, a man who lacks wealth and influence is less likely to have many wives.

(B) They adjusted their initial views on polygamy, recognizing that the experiences of African women should receive closer attention.

(C) Their arguments represented a significant departure from those of Remi Clignet.

(D) Their analyses may have been tainted by the fact that both men practiced polygamy themselves.

(E) Their views reflected the majority opinion of the African population.

3. The passage mentions each of the following, EXCEPT

(A) the year of publication of Remi Clignet's book *Many Wives, Many Powers*

(B) the year in which John Mbiti made a claim that polygamy is an accepted institution

(C) examples of African women's literary productions devoted to family relations

(D) reasons for missionary opposition to polygamy

(E) current-day perspectives with respect to studying polygamy

5

Passage K: Sweet Spot

Most tennis players generally strive to strike the ball on the racket's vibration node, more commonly known as the "sweet spot." How-ever, many players are unaware of the exis-

(5) tence of a second, lesser-known location on the racket face—the center of percussion—that will also greatly diminish the strain on a player's arm when the ball is struck.

In order to understand the physics

(10) of this second sweet spot, it is helpful to consider what would happen to a tennis racket if the player's hand were to vanish at the moment of impact with the ball. The impact of the ball would cause the racket

(15) to bounce backwards, resulting in a trans-lational motion away from the ball. The tendency of this motion would be to jerk all parts of the racket, including the end of its handle, backward, or away from the ball.

(20) Unless the ball happened to hit precisely at the racket's center of mass, the racket would additionally experience a rotational motion around its center of mass—much as a penny that has been struck near its edge

(25) will start to spin. Whenever the ball hits the racket face, the effect of this rotational mo-tion is to jerk the end of the handle forward, towards the ball. Depending on where the ball strikes the racket face, one or the other

(30) of these motions will predominate.

However, there is one point of im-pact, known as the center of percussion, which causes neither motion to predomi-nate; if a ball strikes this point, the impact

(35) does not impart any motion to the end of the handle. The reason for this lack of motion is that the force on the upper part of the hand would be equal and opposite to the force on the lower part

(40) of the hand, resulting in no net force on the tennis player's hand or forearm. The center of percussion constitutes a sec-ond sweet spot because a tennis player's wrist is typically placed next to the end

(45) of the racket's handle. When the player strikes the ball at the center of percus-sion, her wrist is jerked neither forward nor backward, and she experiences greatly reduced vibration in the arm.

(50) The manner in which a tennis player can detect the center of percussion on a given tennis racket follows from the nature of this second sweet spot. The center of percussion can be located via

(55) simple trial and error by holding the end of a tennis racket between the finger and thumb and throwing a ball onto the strings. If the handle jumps out of the player's hand, then the ball has missed

(60) the center of percussion.

1. **The author mentions a penny that has been struck near its edge in order to**

   (A) illustrate what happens at the lesser-known center of percussion

   (B) argue that a penny spins in the exact way that a tennis racket spins

   (C) illustrate the difference between two types of motion

   (D) draw an analogy to help explain a type of motion

   (E) demonstrate that pennies and tennis rackets do not spin in the same way

2. **According to the passage, which of the following occurs when a ball strikes the racket strings on a sweet spot?**

   (A) The jolt that accompanies most strokes will be more pronounced.

   (B) The racket experiences rotational motion but not translational motion.

   (C) The racket experiences translational motion but not rotational motion.

   (D) The player experiences less vibration in the arm holding the racket.

   (E) The center of mass and the center of percussion coincide.

3. **Which of the following can be inferred about the forces acting on the racket handle?**

   (A) A player whose grip is anywhere other than at the end of the racket's handle will experience a jolting sensation when striking the ball.

   (B) Striking a ball at the well-known sweet spot will result in fewer vibrations than striking it at the lesser-known sweet spot.

   (C) Striking a ball on the vibration node will impart some amount of motion to the handle of the racket.

   (D) Depending on where the ball strikes, the handle will experience either translational or rotational motion.

   (E) If the player's hand could disappear at the moment of impact, the racket would drop straight to the ground.

5

Solutions

The solutions show a sample passage map and the point, as well as explanations for each answer choice. No simple story is provided, but you should still be trying to develop that level of understanding of the passage when creating your map. Where appropriate, wrong answers have been labeled by wrong answer category.

Passage I: Japanese Swords

Historians have long recognized the Japanese sword, or *nihonto*, as one of the finest cutting weapons ever produced. But to regard the sword that is synonymous with
(5) the samurai as merely a weapon is to ignore what makes it so special. The Japanese sword has always been considered a splendid weapon and even a spiritual entity. The traditional Japanese adage "the sword is the
(10) soul of the samurai" reflects not only the sword's importance to its wielder but also its permanent connection to its creator, the master smith.

Master smiths may not have been con-
(15) sidered artists in the classical sense, but each smith exerted great care in the process of creating swords, no two of which were ever forged in exactly the same way. Over hundreds of hours, two types of steel were
(20) repeatedly heated, hammered and folded together into thousands of very thin layers, producing a sword with an extremely sharp and durable cutting edge and a flexible, shock-absorbing blade. It was
(25) common, though optional, for a master smith to place a physical signature on a blade; moreover, each smith's secret forging techniques left an idiosyncratic structural signature on his blades. Each
(30) master smith brought a high level of devotion, skill, and attention to detail to the sword-making process, and the sword itself was a reflection of his personal honor and ability. This effort made each blade
(35) as distinctive as the samurai who wielded it such that today the Japanese sword is recognized as much for its artistic merit as for its historical significance.

Sample passage map (yours will likely differ):

① J sword: not just weapon, spirit

② Master smith: skilled
    how to make
    sword: artistic merit, histor signif

The point (articulate to yourself): Japanese sword is a weapon *and* a work of art, important to both samurai and smith. The smiths were almost like artists.

1. **Which of the following can be inferred about the structural signature of a Japanese sword?**

    (A) It is an inscription that the smith places on the blade during the forging process.

    (B) It refers to the particular characteristics of a blade created by a smith's unique forging process.

    (C) It suggests that each blade can be traced back to a known master smith.

    (D) It reflects the soul of the samurai who wielded the sword.

    (E) It refers to the actual curved shape of the blade.

The word *inferred* indicates that this is an inference problem. The question stem references the *structural signature* of the sword. The second paragraph talked about how the smiths forged the swords, so go to that paragraph and scan for the phrase *structural signature*.

The relevant sentence says:

> It was common, though optional, for a master smith to place a physical signature on a blade; moreover, each smith's secret forging techniques left an idiosyncratic structural signature on his blades (lines 24–29).

The sentence references both a physical signature and a structural signature, so the structural signature must not be a literal signature. Further, the sentence indicates that each smith's structural signature is distinctive to the individual (*idiosyncratic*), a result of that smith's secret forging techniques.

(A) This refers to the physical signature, not the structural signature. (True but not right)

(B) CORRECT. This matches the information articulated ahead of time. Each smith's process resulted in a structural signature unique to that smith.

(C) Tricky! The passage does say that a structural signature is unique to one smith, but it does not say that records survive indicating specifically who that smith was. A historian might be able to tell that three blades came from the same smith, but she may not be able to tell who that smith was. (Out of scope)

(D) The first paragraph does include a quote about the soul of the samurai, but this information is not presented in relation to the information about the structural signature. (Mix-up)

(E) Careful: If you have ever seen a samurai sword, then you may remember that it is curved—but the passage doesn't say so! In any case, since the signature is individual to the smith, something that all swords had in common wouldn't be helpful here. (Out of scope)

MANHATTAN
PREP

2. Each of the following is mentioned in the passage EXCEPT

    (A) Every Japanese sword has a unique structure that can be traced back to a special forging process.

    (B) Master smiths kept their forging techniques secret.

    (C) The Japanese sword was considered by some to have a spiritual quality.

    (D) Master smiths are now considered artists by most major historians.

    (E) The Japanese sword is considered both a work of art and a historical artifact.

The question indicates that four of the answers *are* mentioned in the passage, so this is a detail EXCEPT question. The question is too vague to formulate an answer in advance, so go straight to the first answer choice and try to find it in the passage.

(A) True. This is mentioned in the second paragraph (lines 27–29): *each smith's secret forging techniques left an idiosyncratic structural signature on his blades.*

(B) True. This is mentioned in the second paragraph (lines 27–28): *each smith's secret forging techniques.*

(C) True. This is mentioned in the first paragraph (lines 7–8): the *sword has always been considered a splendid weapon and even a spiritual entity.*

(D) CORRECT. False. The passage does not say this. Some people may recognize the smiths as artists (see (E) below), but there is no indication that this view is held by *most major historians.* (Extreme)

(E) True. This is mentioned in the last sentence of the second paragraph (lines 36–38): the *sword is recognized as much for its artistic merit as for its historical significance.*

5

3. The author explains the way in which swords were made in order to

    (A) establish that the Japanese sword is the most important handheld weapon in history

    (B) claim that the skill of the samurai is what made each Japanese sword unique

    (C) support the contention that the master smiths might be considered artists as well as craftsmen

    (D) illustrate that master smiths were more concerned with the artistic merit of their blades than with the blades' practical qualities

    (E) demonstrate that the Japanese sword has more historical importance than artistic importance

The *in order to* language indicates that this is a specific purpose (why) question. Paragraph 2 explains how the swords were made; why did the author include this information?

The beginning and end of the paragraph provide clues. First, the author says that smiths may not have been considered artists in the classical sense, foreshadowing the idea that perhaps they could still be considered artists. The end of the passage indicates that the forging process resulted in such a distinctive blade that the sword is now recognized for its artistic merit as well as its historical significance.

(A) The passage does call the Japanese sword *one of the finest cutting weapons ever produced*, but this is not quite as strong as calling it the most important handheld weapon in history. In any case, this is not the author's purpose in describing how the sword was made. (Extreme)

(B) The passage claims that the smith's secret forging techniques, not the skill of the samurai, made a blade unique. (Direct contradiction)

(C) CORRECT. The default definition for the smiths is craftsmen, but the detailed information about the forging process, as well as the opening and closing sentences, indicate that the smiths might also be considered artists as well.

(D) The passage discusses both the artistic merits and the practical qualities of the swords, but the passage does not indicate whether the smiths thought one was more important than the other. (Out of scope)

(E) The last sentence does talk about both of these concepts, but it does not indicate that one is more important than the other. (Out of scope)

Passage J: Polygamy

Polygamy in Africa has been a popular topic for social research over the past half-century; it has been analyzed by many distinguished minds and in various well-publicized works.
(5) In 1961, when Remi Clignet published his book *Many Wives, Many Powers*, he was not alone in his view that in Africa co-wives may be perceived as direct and indirect sources of increased income and prestige.

(10)   By the 1970s, such arguments had become crystallized and popular. Many other African scholars who wrote on the subject became the new champions of this philosophy. For example, in 1983, John Mbiti pro-
(15) claimed that polygamy is an accepted and respectable institution serving many useful social purposes. Similarly, G.K. Nukunya, in his paper "Polygamy as a Symbol of Status," reiterated Mbiti's idea that a plurality of
(20) wives is a legitimate sign of affluence and power in the African society.

The colonial missionary voice, however, provided consistent opposition to polygamy. Invoking the authority of the Bible, mission-
(25) aries argued that the practice was unethical and destructive of family life, and they propagated the view that Africans had to be coerced into abiding by the monogamous view of marriage favored by West-
(30) ern culture. In some instances, missionaries even dictated immediate divorce for newly-converted men who had already entered into polygamous marriages. Unfortunately, neither the missionary
(35) voice nor the scholarly voice considered the views of African women important. Although there was some awareness that women regarded polygamy as both a curse and a blessing, the distanced, albeit
(40) scientific, perspective of an outside observer predominated both at the pulpit and in scholarly writings.

Contemporary research in the social sciences has begun to focus on
(45) the protagonist's voice in the study of culture, recognizing that the views and experiences of those who take part in a given reality ought to receive close examination. This privileging of
(50) the protagonist seems appropriate, particularly given that women in Africa have often used literary productions to comment on marriage, family, and gender relations.

Sample passage map (yours will likely differ):

① *Polyg Afr*
   '61 Clignet: P = income, prestige
② *70s, 80s: positive dtls*
③ *Missionary: against*
   neither listened to women
④ *Now: listening to women*

The point (articulate to yourself): Early scholars thought polygamy was a good thing. Missionaries were against it. Now, people are actually paying attention to what the women think.

1. According to the passage, colonial missionaries and popular scholars shared which of the following traits in their approach to the issue of polygamy?

(A) Both considered polygamy a sign of social status and success.

(B) Neither accounted for the views of local women.

(C) Both attempted to limit the prevalence of polygamy.

(D) Both pointed out polygamy's destructive effects on family life.

(E) Both exhibited a somewhat negative attitude towards polygamy.

The language *according to the passage* indicates that this is a detail question. In general, the scholars' view was positive while the missionaries' view was negative, so these two groups would not appear to have many traits in common. The missionary is not mentioned until the third paragraph, so begin searching there.

Halfway through the third paragraph, the author states that *neither the missionary voice nor the scholarly voice considered the views of African women important.*

(A) This represents the position of the scholars, but not the missionaries. (Direct contradiction)

(B) CORRECT. This choice matches the relevant sentence from the passage.

(C) and (D) Both of these choices describe things that the missionaries did. The passage provides no information on this topic with respect to the scholars; the scholars, though, had a positive view of polygamy. (Out of scope)

(E) The scholars cited had a positive attitude towards polygamy. (Direct contradiction)

2. The author implies which of the following about Nukunya and Mbiti's works?

(A) From their point of view, a man who lacks wealth and influence is less likely to have many wives.

(B) They adjusted their initial views on polygamy, recognizing that the experiences of African women should receive closer attention.

(C) Their arguments represented a significant departure from those of Remi Clignet.

(D) Their analyses may have been tainted by the fact that both men practiced polygamy themselves.

(E) Their views reflected the majority opinion of the African population.

The word *implies* indicates that this is an inference question. The two scholars mentioned were discussed in the second paragraph.

Both had positive views of polygamy. The question asks about both Mbiti and Nukunya's views, and only one view is attributed to both: Nukunya agreed with Mbiti's idea that polygamy is a *sign of affluence and power in the African society*. The correct answer will be something that follows from that information.

(A) **CORRECT.** If polygamy leads to affluence and power, then someone who does not have those two things is less likely to be practicing polygamy.

(B) The passage does not indicate that they adjusted their views. In fact, the third paragraph says that the *scholarly voice* did not consider women's views important. (Direct contradiction)

(C) Clignet was pro-polygamy, as were Mbiti and Nukunya; their views were not different from Clignet's. (Direct contradiction)

(D) The passage does not indicate whether the two men practiced polygamy themselves. (Out of scope)

(E) The passage indicates only that polygamy in Africa has been a popular research topic. The passage does not indicate whether a majority of Africans supported polygamy or considered it in a positive light. (Out of scope)

3. The passage mentions each of the following, EXCEPT

(A) the year of publication of Remi Clignet's book *Many Wives, Many Powers*

(B) the year in which John Mbiti made a claim that polygamy is an accepted institution

(C) examples of African women's literary productions devoted to family relations

(D) reasons for missionary opposition to polygamy

(E) current-day perspectives with respect to studying polygamy

The question indicates that four of the answers *are* mentioned in the passage, so this is a detail EXCEPT question. The question is too vague to formulate an answer in advance, so go straight to the first answer choice and try to find it in the passage.

(A) True. Clignet's book was published in 1961 (line 5).

(B) True. Mbiti made this claim in 1983 (lines 14–16).

(C) **CORRECT.** Though the passage does mention that African women used literary productions in certain ways, it is false that the passage gives any examples of this.

(D) True. The second sentence of paragraph three provides specific reasons that the missionaries opposed polygamy.

(E) True. The final paragraph indicates that contemporary research has finally begun to recognize that it is important to focus on the voices of those who are actually in polygamous marriages, including women.

Passage K: Sweet Spot

Most tennis players generally strive to strike the ball on the racket's vibration node, more commonly known as the "sweet spot." However, many players are unaware of the exis-
(5) tence of a second, lesser-known location on the racket face—the center of percussion—that will also greatly diminish the strain on a player's arm when the ball is struck.

In order to understand the physics
(10) of this second sweet spot, it is helpful to consider what would happen to a tennis racket if the player's hand were to vanish at the moment of impact with the ball. The impact of the ball would cause the racket
(15) to bounce backwards, resulting in a translational motion away from the ball. The tendency of this motion would be to jerk all parts of the racket, including the end of its handle, backward, or away from the ball.
(20) Unless the ball happened to hit precisely at the racket's center of mass, the racket would additionally experience a rotational motion around its center of mass—much as a penny that has been struck near its edge
(25) will start to spin. Whenever the ball hits the racket face, the effect of this rotational motion is to jerk the end of the handle forward, towards the ball. Depending on where the ball strikes the racket face, one or the other
(30) of these motions will predominate.

However, there is one point of impact, known as the center of percussion, which causes neither motion to predominate; if a ball strikes this point, the impact
(35) does not impart any motion to the end of the handle. The reason for this lack of motion is that the force on the upper part of the hand would be equal and opposite to the force on the lower part
(40) of the hand, resulting in no net force on the tennis player's hand or forearm. The center of percussion constitutes a second sweet spot because a tennis player's wrist is typically placed next to the end
(45) of the racket's handle. When the player strikes the ball at the center of percussion, her wrist is jerked neither forward nor backward, and she experiences greatly reduced vibration in the arm.

(50) The manner in which a tennis player can detect the center of percussion on a given tennis racket follows from the nature of this second sweet spot. The center of percussion can be located via
(55) simple trial and error by holding the end of a tennis racket between the finger and thumb and throwing a ball onto the strings. If the handle jumps out of the player's hand, then the ball has missed
(60) the center of percussion.

Sample passage map (yours will likely differ):

Sweet Spot

① *2 sweet spots – one less known*
   SS = reduce strain
② *if hand disappeared?*
   dtl...
③ *center percuss = "lack of motion"*
   <<< vibration
④ *how to find center percuss*

The point (articulate to yourself): People know about one sweet spot but not the other. Both reduce vibration in the arm. (Plus lots of technical details—ignore for now!)

1. The author mentions a penny that has been struck near its edge in order to

   (A) illustrate what happens at the lesser-known center of percussion

   (B) argue that a penny spins in the exact way that a tennis racket spins

   (C) illustrate the difference between two types of motion

   (D) draw an analogy to help explain a type of motion

   (E) demonstrate that pennies and tennis rackets do not spin in the same way

The *in order to* language indicates that this is a specific purpose (why) question. Paragraph two mentions the penny; why did the author include this information?

Here's the relevant text:

> Unless the ball happened to hit precisely at the racket's center of mass, the racket would additionally experience a rotational motion around its center of mass—much as a penny that has been struck near its edge will start to spin.

The first part of the sentence talks about a certain motion that the tennis racket experiences. After the dash, the *much as a penny* language indicates that this example is an analogy: the racket is spinning in the same way that the penny would spin.

(A) This choice is tricky. The beginning of the third paragraph indicates that the motion described at the end of the second paragraph is not what happens at the center of percussion. Even if you miss that, it's enough to find another answer choice that does match your pre-stated idea. (Direct contradiction)

(B) The author is trying to draw a parallel between the two, but does not say that they spin in the *exact* same way. (Extreme)

(C) The paragraph does talk about two types of motion, but the penny example applies just to one of them. (True but not right)

(D) CORRECT. The penny analogy explains how the tennis racket spins.

(E) The analogy is based on a similarity in the way that they spin. (Direct contradiction)

2. According to the passage, which of the following occurs when a ball strikes the racket strings on a sweet spot?

(A) The jolt that accompanies most strokes will be more pronounced.

(B) The racket experiences rotational motion but not translational motion.

(C) The racket experiences translational motion but not rotational motion.

(D) The player experiences less vibration in the arm holding the racket.

(E) The center of mass and the center of percussion coincide.

The language *according to the passage* indicates that this is a detail question. A large portion of the passage talks about what happens when a ball strikes a racket on a sweet spot. Where should you look?

When the question is this broad, find the first mention of the topic. This first mention will give you the main idea and you can eliminate some answers. If you cannot eliminate all four, then you can go to the next mention of the topic and use that to eliminate until you get down to one answer (or you decide that you'd rather guess and move on).

The first paragraph indicates that there are two sweet spots and that striking a ball there will *greatly diminish the strain on a player's arm.*

(A) This goes against the basic idea that the strain will decrease. (Direct contradiction)

(B) and (C) The second paragraph does talk about these two forces. Before you dive into these details, check the remaining answers to see whether one matches your predicted answer.

(D) CORRECT. This is the basic benefit of the sweet spot: when a player hits a ball there, the strain, or vibration, felt in the arm is lessened.

(E) The passage does mention both the center of percussion and the center of mass. Because answer (D) already works, dismiss this answer.

In the case of answers (B), (C), and (E), the test writer is trying to slow you down. You aren't required to assess each answer choice in order; when you hit something that requires a deeper dive, feel free to check the other answer choices first.

Striking the ball at a sweet spot can result in both translational and rotational motion, so answers (B) and (C) are both wrong. The passage never indicates a time when the center of mass and center of percussion would be in the same location, so answer (E) is also wrong.

3. Which of the following can be inferred about the forces acting on the racket handle?

(A) A player whose grip is anywhere other than at the end of the racket's handle will experience a jolting sensation when striking the ball.

(B) Striking a ball at the well-known sweet spot will result in fewer vibrations than striking it at the lesser-known sweet spot.

(C) Striking a ball on the vibration node will impart some amount of motion to the handle of the racket.

(D) Depending on where the ball strikes, the handle will experience either translational or rotational motion.

(E) If the player's hand could disappear at the moment of impact, the racket would drop straight to the ground.

The word *inferred* indicates that this is an inference question. The forces acting on the racket handle are first discussed in paragraph two.

If you like the topic, feel free to delve into the technical details. If you don't, summarize only the high-level points (or guess and move on!). Remember that the question asks specifically about the racket handle. Translational motion moves the racket handle backward. Rotational motion jerks the handle forward.

The third paragraph adds that if a ball strikes the center of percussion, there will be no motion at the end of the handle.

(A) The passage does not address what would happen if the player gripped the racket somewhere other than the end of the handle. The "sweet spot" describes where the ball strikes the strings, not where the player holds the racket. (Out of scope)

(B) The passage does not address which sweet spot might result in fewer vibrations. (Out of scope)

(C) CORRECT. This is a very tricky answer! The third paragraph indicates that striking the ball at the center of percussion will result in no motion—and the author specifies that this lack of motion occurs only when the ball is struck at this one location. If the ball strikes any *other* point on the racket, then the handle will experience some motion. The vibration node is the well-known sweet spot (see the first paragraph), so it qualifies as a spot other than the center of percussion.

(D) If the ball is struck at the center of percussion, it will experience neither type of motion. If the ball is struck elsewhere, it will experience both types of motion. (Direct contradiction)

(E) The second paragraph states that, if the player's hand somehow disappeared, then the racket would bounce backwards, among other motions. (Direct contradiction)

This last problem was incredibly hard. Even if you didn't find the support for (C), congratulate yourself if you were able to eliminate most or all of the incorrect answers! Also, notice that the second question, while also a detail question, was easier to answer because it did not require as much technical understanding of the passage. If you are having trouble following a very technical passage, you may get lucky and be offered a specific question that you can answer with only a high-level understanding. However, it's likely that at least one question will require enough technical understanding that you may just want to guess quickly and move on.

5

Chapter 6 of

Reading Comprehension

Extra Problem Set

In This Chapter...

Extra Problem Set

Chapter 6

Extra Problem Set

Time to put it all together! This chapter contains four passages with either four or five accompanying questions each. (Note: The real test will give you either three or four questions per passage.)

Each title is followed by an ideal length of time to give yourself to complete the passage and all questions. You can, of course, choose to spend extra time—but on the real test, that time will have to come from other questions. (If you receive extended time on the test, adjust accordingly.)

Passage L: The Invention of TV (8 minutes)

In the early years of television, Vladimir Zworykin was considered the device's inventor, at least publicly. His loudest champion was his boss, David Sarnoff, then president of RCA (5) and a man regarded even today as "the father of television." Current historians agree, however, that Philo Farnsworth, a self-educated prodigy who was the first to transmit live images, was television's technical inventor.

(10)   In his own time, Farnsworth's contributions went largely unnoticed, in large part because he was excluded from the process of introducing the invention to a national audience. Sarnoff put televisions into living (15) rooms, and Sarnoff was responsible for a dominant paradigm of the television industry that continues to be relevant today: advertisers pay for the programming so that they can have a receptive audience for their products. (20) Sarnoff had already utilized this construct to develop the radio industry, and it had, within ten years, become ubiquitous. Farnsworth thought the television should be used as an educational tool, but he (25) had little understanding of the business world, and was never able to implement his ideas.

    Some argue that Sarnoff simply adapted the business model for radio (30) and television from the newspaper industry, replacing the revenue from subscriptions and newsstand purchases with that of television set sales, but Sarnoff promoted himself as nothing less than a (35) visionary. Some television critics argue that the construct Sarnoff implemented has played a negative role in determining the content of the programs themselves, while others contend that it merely cre- (40) ated a democratic platform from which the audience can determine the types of programming it desires.

1. The primary purpose of the passage is to

    (A) correct public misconceptions about Farnsworth's role in developing early television programs

    (B) debate the influence of television on popular culture

    (C) challenge the current public perception of Vladimir Zworykin

    (D) chronicle the events that led from the development of radio to the invention of the television

    (E) describe Sarnoff's influence on the public perception of television's inception and the debate around the impact of Sarnoff's paradigm

6

2. Which of the following best illustrates the relationship between the second and third paragraphs?

    (A) The second paragraph dissects the evolution of a contemporary controversy; the third paragraph presents differing viewpoints on that controversy.

    (B) The second paragraph explores the antithetical intentions of two men involved in the infancy of an industry; the third paragraph details the eventual deterioration of that industry.

    (C) The second paragraph presents differing views of a historical event; the third paragraph represents the author's personal opinion about that event.

    (D) The second paragraph provides details that are necessary to support the author's opinion, which is presented in the third paragraph.

    (E) The second paragraph presents divergent visions about the implementation of a technology; the third paragraph further explores one of those perspectives.

3. According to the passage, the television industry, at its inception, earned revenue from

    (A) advertising only

    (B) advertising and the sale of television sets

    (C) advertising and subscriptions

    (D) subscriptions and the sale of television sets

    (E) advertising, subscriptions, and the sale of television sets

4. The passage suggests that Farnsworth might have earned greater public notoriety for his invention if

    (A) Vladimir Zworykin had been less vocal about his own contributions to the television

    (B) Farnsworth had been able to develop and air his own educational programs

    (C) Farnsworth had involved Sarnoff in his plans to develop, manufacture, or distribute the television

    (D) Sarnoff had involved Farnsworth in his plans to develop, manufacture, or distribute the television

    (E) Farnsworth had conducted research into the type of programming the audience most wanted to watch

6

Passage M: Life on Mars (7 minutes)

Because of the proximity and likeness of Mars to Earth, scientists have long speculated about the possibility of life on Mars. As early as the mid-seventeenth cen-
(5) tury, astronomers observed polar ice caps on Mars, and by the mid-nineteenth century, scientists discovered other similarities to Earth, including the length of day and axial tilt. But in 1965, photos taken by the Mari-
(10) ner 4 probe revealed a Mars without rivers, oceans or signs of life. Moreover, in the 1990s, it was discovered that Mars, unlike Earth, no longer possessed a substantial global magnetic field, allowing celestial radiation
(15) to reach the planet's surface and solar wind to eliminate much of Mars's atmosphere over the course of several billion years.

More recent probes have investigated
(20) whether there was once liquid water on Mars. Some scientists believe that this question is definitively answered by the presence of certain geological landforms. Others posit that alternative explana-
(25) tions, such as wind erosion or carbon dioxide oceans, may be responsible for these formations. Mars rovers *Opportunity* and *Spirit*, which began exploring the surface of Mars in 2004, have both
(30) discovered geological evidence of past water activity. In 2013, the rover *Curiosity* found evidence that the soil on the surface of Mars is approximately 2% water by weight. These findings substantially
(35) bolster claims that there was once life on Mars.

1. The passage is primarily concerned with which of the following?

    (A) Disproving a widely accepted theory

    (B) Initiating a debate about an unproven theory

    (C) Presenting evidence in support of a recently-formulated claim

    (D) Describing various discoveries made concerning the possibility of life on Mars

    (E) Detailing the findings of the Mars rovers *Opportunity*, *Spirit*, and *Curiosity*

2. Each of the following discoveries is mentioned in the passage EXCEPT:

    (A) Wind erosion and carbon dioxide oceans are responsible for certain geological landforms on Mars.

    (B) Mars does not have a substantial global magnetic field.

    (C) Mars had water activity at some point in the past.

    (D) The length of day on Mars is similar to that on Earth.

    (E) The axial tilt of Mars is similar to that of Earth.

6

3. The passage suggests which of the following about polar ice caps?

    (A) Until recently, the ones on Mars were thought to consist largely of carbon dioxide.

    (B) The ones on Mars are made almost entirely of frozen water.

    (C) They are also found on Earth.

    (D) Their formation is tied to length of day and axial tilt.

    (E) They indicate that conditions on the planet Mars were once very different than they are at present.

4. It can be inferred from the passage that scientists would be more likely to suspect that Mars once held life if there were evidence of which of the following features?

    (A) Carbon dioxide oceans

    (B) Celestial radiation and solar wind

    (C) High daily level of sunlight reaching the planet's surface

    (D) Volcanic eruptions

    (E) A significant global magnetic field

6

Passage N: Fossils (8.5 minutes)

In archaeology, as in the physical sciences, new discoveries frequently undermine accepted findings and give rise to new theories. This trend can be seen in the reaction to the
(5) recent discovery of a set of 3.3-million-year-old fossils in Ethiopia, the remains of the earliest well-preserved child ever found. The fossilized child was estimated to be about 3 years old at death, female, and a member
(10) of the *Australopithecus afarensis* species. The *afarensis* species, a major human ancestor, lived in Africa from earlier than 3.7 million to 3 million years ago. "Her completeness, antiquity, and age at death make this find
(15) unprecedented in the history of paleoanthropology," said Zeresenay Alemseged, a noted paleoanthropologist. Other scientists said that the discovery could reconfigure conceptions about the lives and capacities of these
(20) early humans.

Prior to this discovery, it had been thought that the *afarensis* species had abandoned the arboreal habitat of its ape cousins. However, while the lower
(25) limbs of this fossil supported findings that *afarensis* walked upright, its gorilla-like arms and shoulders suggested that it retained the ability to swing through trees. This has initiated a reexamination
(30) of many accepted theories of early human development. Also, the presence of a hyoid bone, a rarely preserved bone in the larynx that supports muscles of the throat, has had a tremendous impact on
(35) theories about the origins of speech. The fossil bone is primitive and more similar to that of apes than to that of humans, but it is the first hyoid found in such an early human-related
(40) species.

1. The primary purpose of the passage is to

    (A) discuss a controversial scientific discovery

    (B) contrast varying theories of human development

    (C) support a general contention with a specific example

    (D) argue for the importance of a particular field of study

    (E) refute a popular misconception

2. The passage quotes Zeresenay Alemseged in order to

    (A) qualify the main idea of the first paragraph

    (B) provide contrast to the claims of other scientists

    (C) support the theory regarding the linguistic abilities of the *afarensis* species

    (D) support the stated significance of the discovery

    (E) provide a subjective opinion that is refuted in the second paragraph

3. It can be inferred from the passage's description of the discovery of the fossil hyoid bone that

(A) *Australopithecus afarensis* was capable of speech

(B) the discovered hyoid bone is less primitive than the hyoid bone of apes

(C) the hyoid bone is necessary for speech

(D) the discovery of the hyoid bone necessitated the reexamination of prior theories

(E) the hyoid bone was the most important fossil found at the site

4. Each of the following is cited as a reason that the fossils discovered in Ethiopia were important EXCEPT

(A) the fact that the remains were those of a child

(B) the age of the fossils

(C) the location of the discovery

(D) the presence of a bone not usually discovered

(E) the intact nature of the fossils

5. The impact of the discovery of the hyoid bone in the field of archaeology is most closely analogous to which of the following situations?

(A) The discovery and analysis of cosmic rays lend support to a widely accepted theory of the origin of the universe.

(B) The original manuscript of a deceased nineteenth-century author confirms ideas about the development of an important work of literature.

(C) The continued prosperity of a state-run economy stirs debate in the discipline of macroeconomics.

(D) Newly revealed journal entries by a prominent Civil War–era politician lead to a questioning of certain accepted historical interpretations about the conflict.

(E) Research into the mapping of the human genome gives rise to nascent applications of individually tailored medicines.

6

Passage O: Chaos Theory (8.5 minutes)

Around 1960, mathematician Edward Lorenz found unexpected behavior in apparently simple equations representing atmospheric air flows. Whenever he reran his model with
(5) the same inputs, different outputs resulted, although the model lacked any random elements. Lorenz realized that tiny rounding errors in the initial data mushroomed over time, leading to erratic results. His findings
(10) marked a seminal moment in the development of chaos theory, which, despite its name, has little to do with randomness.

Lorenz's experiment was one of the first to demonstrate conclusively that unpredict-
(15) ability can arise from deterministic equations, which do not involve chance outcomes. In order to understand this phenomenon, first consider the non-chaotic system of two poppy seeds placed in a round bowl. As the seeds
(20) roll to the bowl's center, a position known as a point attractor, the distance between the seeds shrinks. If, instead, the bowl is flipped over, two seeds placed on top will roll away from each other. Such a system, while still not
(25) technically chaotic, enlarges initial differences in position.

Chaotic systems, such as a machine mixing bread dough, are characterized by both attraction and repulsion. As the dough is
(30) stretched, folded, and pressed back together, any poppy seeds sprinkled in are intermixed seemingly at random. But this randomness is illusory. In fact, the poppy seeds are captured by "strange attrac-
(35) tors," staggeringly complex pathways whose tangles appear accidental but are in fact determined by the system's fundamental equations.

During the dough-kneading process,
(40) two poppy seeds positioned next to each other eventually go their separate ways. Any early divergence or measurement error is repeatedly amplified by the mixing until the position of any seed becomes
(45) effectively unpredictable. It is this "sensitive dependence on initial conditions" and not true randomness that generates unpredictability in chaotic systems, of which one example may be the Earth's
(50) weather. According to the popular interpretation of the "Butterfly Effect," a butterfly flapping its wings causes hurricanes. A better understanding is that the butterfly causes uncertainty about the
(55) precise state of the air. This microscopic uncertainty grows until it encompasses even hurricanes. Few meteorologists believe that we will ever be able to predict rain or shine for a particular day years in
(60) the future.

1. **The primary purpose of this passage is to**

(A) explain how non-random systems can produce unpredictable results

(B) trace the historical development of a scientific theory

(C) distinguish one theory from its opposite

(D) describe the spread of a technical model from one field of study to others

(E) contrast possible causes of weather phenomena

2. According to the passage, what is true about poppy seeds in bread dough, once the dough has been thoroughly mixed?

(A) They have been individually stretched and folded over, like miniature versions of the entire dough.

(B) They are scattered in random clumps throughout the dough.

(C) They are accidentally caught in tangled objects called strange attractors.

(D) They are bound to regularly dispersed patterns of point attractors.

(E) They are in positions dictated by the underlying equations that govern the mixing process.

3. According to the passage, the small rounding errors in Lorenz's model

(A) rendered the results unusable for the purposes of scientific research

(B) were deliberately included to represent tiny fluctuations in atmospheric air currents

(C) had a surprisingly large impact over time

(D) were at least partially expected, given the complexity of the actual atmosphere

(E) shrank to insignificant levels during each trial of the model

4. The passage mentions each of the following as an example or potential example of a chaotic or non-chaotic system EXCEPT

(A) a dough-mixing machine

(B) atmospheric weather patterns

(C) poppy seeds placed on top of an upside-down bowl

(D) poppy seeds placed in a right-side-up bowl

(E) fluctuating butterfly flight patterns

6

Solutions

The solutions show a sample passage map and the point, as well as explanations for each answer choice. Where appropriate, wrong answers have been labeled by wrong answer category.

Passage L: The Invention of TV

In the early years of television, Vladimir Zworykin was considered the device's inventor, at least publicly. His loudest champion was his boss, David Sarnoff, then president of RCA
(5) and a man regarded even today as "the father of television." Current historians agree, however, that Philo Farnsworth, a self-educated prodigy who was the first to transmit live images, was television's technical inventor.
(10) In his own time, Farnsworth's contributions went largely unnoticed, in large part because he was excluded from the process of introducing the invention to a national audience. Sarnoff put televisions into living
(15) rooms, and Sarnoff was responsible for a dominant paradigm of the television industry that continues to be relevant today: advertisers pay for the programming so that they can have a receptive audience for their products.
(20) Sarnoff had already utilized this construct to develop the radio industry, and it had,

within ten years, become ubiquitous. Farnsworth thought the television should be used as an educational tool, but he
(25) had little understanding of the business world, and was never able to implement his ideas.

Some argue that Sarnoff simply adapted the business model for radio
(30) and television from the newspaper industry, replacing the revenue from subscriptions and newsstand purchases with that of television set sales, but Sarnoff promoted himself as nothing less than a
(35) visionary. Some television critics argue that the construct Sarnoff implemented has played a negative role in determining the content of the programs themselves, while others contend that it merely cre-
(40) ated a democratic platform from which the audience can determine the types of programming it desires.

6

Sample passage map (yours will likely differ):

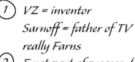

   1 *VZ = inventor*
      Sarnoff = father of TV
      really Farns
   2 *F not part of process, focus edu*
      S made commercial (same as radio)
   3 *S just adapted? or visionary?*
      some see S as neg, some pos

The point (articulate to yourself): Farnsworth really invented TV, but he didn't know how to turn it into a business. Sarnoff used the radio model to make television big business. People have differing feelings about his role.

1. The primary purpose of the passage is to

(A) correct public misconceptions about Farnsworth's role in developing early television programs

(B) debate the influence of television on popular culture

(C) challenge the current public perception of Vladimir Zworykin

(D) chronicle the events that led from the development of radio to the invention of the television

(E) describe Sarnoff's influence on the public perception of television's inception and the debate around the impact of Sarnoff's paradigm

The wording indicates that this is a primary purpose question. Glance at your map and remind yourself of the point before you go to the answers.

(A) The passage does correct the misconception about Farnsworth's role. This is only a detail of the passage, however; most of the passage talks about Sarnoff's development of the business model for television. (True but not right)

(B) The passage does not delve into popular culture. (Out of scope)

(C) Zworykin is not the focus of the passage, nor does the passage say anything about *current* public perception of Zworykin; it only indicates that he was once considered the inventor of the technology. (Out of scope)

(D) The passage is not about the events that led to the invention of television, nor is it about radio. Radio is only mentioned because Sarnoff used a similar business model to launch the business of television. (Out of scope)

(E) CORRECT. The passage does describe how Sarnoff made television popular; some critics think his role was positive while others think it was negative. Notice that this is the only answer choice that mentions Sarnoff. He is featured prominently in every paragraph, so any answer choice representing the point of the passage should not mention other people while ignoring him!

2. Which of the following best illustrates the relationship between the second and third paragraphs?

(A) The second paragraph dissects the evolution of a contemporary controversy; the third paragraph presents differing viewpoints on that controversy.

(B) The second paragraph explores the antithetical intentions of two men involved in the infancy of an industry; the third paragraph details the eventual deterioration of that industry.

(C) The second paragraph presents differing views of a historical event; the third paragraph represents the author's personal opinion about that event.

(D) The second paragraph provides details that are necessary to support the author's opinion, which is presented in the third paragraph.

(E) The second paragraph presents divergent visions about a new technology; the third paragraph further explores one of those perspectives.

This is a paragraph question. Glance at your map and articulate to yourself the relationship between the second and third paragraphs before you check the answers.

The second paragraph explains how Sarnoff made television a commercial success, and why Farnsworth was not able to do so. The third paragraph expands on Sarnoff's work, indicating both positive and negative views.

(A) Perhaps the fact that the wrong man was initially credited with television's invention could be considered a controversy, but that controversy is not contemporary, nor is it the purpose of the second or third paragraphs. (Out of scope)

(B) The second paragraph might be described in this way, but the third paragraph does not talk about the deterioration of television. Rather, the industry was (and is!) a success. Perhaps it didn't live up to Farnsworth's hopes, but the passage doesn't describe any decline—in fact, Farnsworth's vision didn't get off the ground. (Direct contradiction)

(C) The second paragraph provides historical details of the launch of television, not different views of the launch. The third paragraph does not present the author's personal opinion. (Out of scope)

(D) The author does not provide his own opinion; rather, he conveys the opinions of others. (Out of scope)

(E) CORRECT. The second paragraph does present the two different visions held by Farnsworth and Sarnoff. The third paragraph does provide additional information about Sarnoff's particular vision.

3. According to the passage, the television industry, at its inception, earned revenue from

(A) advertising only

(B) advertising and the sale of television sets

(C) advertising and subscriptions

(D) subscriptions and the sale of television sets

(E) advertising, subscriptions, and the sale of television sets

The language *according to the passage* indicates that this is a detail question. The passage discusses television revenues in the second and third paragraphs. Search for the information.

Paragraph 2 (lines 18–19): *advertisers pay for the programming*

Paragraph 3 (lines 32–34): *replacing the revenue from subscriptions and newsstand purchases with that of television set sales*

(A) Revenue was also earned from the sale of TV sets. (True but not right)

(B) CORRECT. Revenue was earned from advertisers and the sale of TV sets.

(C), (D), (E) Subscriptions were used in the newspaper industry. (Mix-up)

4. The passage suggests that Farnsworth might have earned greater public notoriety for his invention if

(A) Vladimir Zworykin had been less vocal about his own contributions to the television

(B) Farnsworth had been able to develop and air his own educational programs

(C) Farnsworth had involved Sarnoff in his plans to develop, manufacture, or distribute the television

(D) Sarnoff had involved Farnsworth in his plans to develop, manufacture, or distribute the television

(E) Farnsworth had conducted research into the type of programming the audience most wanted to watch

The word *suggests* signals that this is an inference question, so you will need to go back to the passage. Farnsworth's contributions are discussed in the second paragraph.

[Farnsworth] *was excluded from the process of introducing the invention to a national audience … Farnsworth thought the television should be used as an educational tool, but he had little understanding of the business world, and was never able to implement his ideas* (lines 13–28).

If Farnsworth hadn't been excluded, maybe he would have earned more acclaim. Alternatively, if he had understood business better, then he might have earned more acclaim. Look for an answer with a similar meaning.

(A) The passage says that Sarnoff, not Zworykin himself, was vocal about Zworykin's contributions. (Mix-up)

(B) It's possible that if Farnsworth had been able to follow through on his goal of using television for education, he would have earned public acclaim, but the passage says nothing to indicate this. Because he had little understanding of business, his programs might not have been great successes even if he had been able to produce them. (Out of scope)

(C) There is no indication that Farnsworth had any such plans. Rather, it would have helped Farnsworth to be involved with Sarnoff's plans. (Mix-up)

(D) CORRECT. If Farnsworth hadn't been excluded, then he might have garnered acclaim as Sarnoff and Zworykin did.

(E) The passage indicates that Farnsworth had little understanding of the business world; even if he knew what audiences wanted to watch, he wouldn't necessarily have known how to build a successful business model. (Out of scope)

Passage M: Life on Mars

Because of the proximity and likeness of Mars to Earth, scientists have long speculated about the possibility of life on Mars. As early as the mid-seventeenth cen-
(5) tury, astronomers observed polar ice caps on Mars, and by the mid-nineteenth century, scientists discovered other similarities to Earth, including the length of day and axial tilt. But in 1965, photos taken by the Mari-
(10) ner 4 probe revealed a Mars without rivers, oceans or signs of life. Moreover, in the 1990s, it was discovered that Mars, unlike Earth, no longer possessed a substantial global magnetic field, allowing celestial radiation
(15) to reach the planet's surface and solar wind to eliminate much of Mars's atmosphere over the course of several billion years.

More recent probes have investigated
(20) whether there was once liquid water on Mars. Some scientists believe that this question is definitively answered by the presence of certain geological landforms. Others posit that alternative explana-
(25) tions, such as wind erosion or carbon dioxide oceans, may be responsible for these formations. Mars rovers *Opportunity* and *Spirit*, which began exploring the surface of Mars in 2004, have both
(30) discovered geological evidence of past water activity. In 2013, the rover *Curiosity* found evidence that the soil on the surface of Mars is approximately 2% water by weight. These findings substantially
(35) bolster claims that there was once life on Mars.

Sample passage map (yours will likely differ):

Life on Mars

① *Life on Mars?*
  + sim to Earth
  – diff too
② *Water?*
  debate
  recent: yes, water

The point (articulate to yourself): Debate about life on Mars. Positives and negatives but the big deal was the discovery of water, increasing the chance that there was life on Mars.

1. The passage is primarily concerned with which of the following?

(A) Disproving a widely accepted theory

(B) Initiating a debate about an unproven theory

(C) Presenting evidence in support of a recently formulated claim

(D) Describing various discoveries made concerning the possibility of life on Mars

(E) Detailing the findings of the Mars rovers *Opportunity, Spirit,* and *Curiosity*

This is a primary purpose question. Glance at your map and remind yourself of the point before you go to the answers.

(A) There is no widely accepted theory, just speculation. Plus, that speculation is more positive than negative! (Out of scope)

(B) The passage does discuss a potential theory (that there may once have been life on Mars), but the passage itself does not initiate any debate. Rather, it reports on various findings and opinions of others. (Out of scope)

(C) The earliest mentioned interest in Mars was in the mid-seventeenth century; this is not recent. (One word off)

(D) CORRECT. The passage does describe various discoveries made in the mid-seventeenth and mid-nineteenth centuries, as well as more recently, concerning the possibility of life on Mars.

(E) The passage does discuss this, but the rovers are passage detail; they are not the overall point of the passage. (True but not right)

2. Each of the following discoveries is mentioned in the passage EXCEPT

    (A) wind erosion and carbon dioxide oceans are responsible for certain geological landforms on Mars

    (B) Mars does not have a substantial global magnetic field

    (C) Mars had water activity at some point in the past

    (D) the length of day on Mars is similar to that on Earth

    (E) the axial tilt of Mars is similar to that of Earth

The question indicates that four of the answers *are* mentioned in the passage, so this is a detail EXCEPT question. The entire passage is about discoveries, so go straight to the first answer choice and try to find it in the passage.

    (A) CORRECT. The passage says only that wind erosion or carbon dioxide *may* be responsible for certain geological landforms, not that they *are*. This is an unusual form of an Extreme answer: though the word *are* is not an extreme word itself, it is more extreme than *may*. (Extreme)

    (B) True. The first paragraph says that Mars *no longer possessed a global magnetic field* (lines 13–14).

    (C) True. The second paragraph says that *Mars rovers Opportunity and Spirit … discovered geological evidence of past water activity* (lines 27–31).

    (D) True. The first paragraph states that *scientists discovered similarities to Earth, including the length of day* (lines 7–8).

    (E) True. The first paragraph states that *scientists discovered similarities to Earth, including the … axial tilt* (lines 7–9).

3. The passage suggests which of the following about polar ice caps?

    (A) Until recently, the ones on Mars were thought to consist largely of carbon dioxide.

    (B) The ones on Mars are made almost entirely of frozen water.

    (C) They are also found on Earth.

    (D) Their formation is tied to length of day and axial tilt.

    (E) They indicate that conditions on the planet Mars were once very different than they are at present.

The word *suggests* points to an inference question. The passage mentions polar ice caps in the first paragraph:

> *As early as the mid-seventeenth century, astronomers observed polar ice caps on Mars, and by the mid-nineteenth century, scientists discovered other similarities to Earth, including the length of day and axial tilt* (lines 4–9).

The second half of the sentence states that scientists discovered *other* similarities to Earth, implying that polar ice caps are also a similarity between the two planets.

(A) The passage does mention carbon dioxide, but not in the context of polar ice caps. (Mix-up)

(B) The passage does not provide any information about the content of polar ice caps. (Out of scope)

(C) CORRECT. The sentence says that scientists discovered *other* similarities to Earth, implying that the earlier discovery (polar ice caps) is also similar to what is found on Earth.

(D) The passage mentions length of day and axial tilt as examples of other similarities to Earth, but it does not indicate that those had anything to do with the formation of polar ice caps. (Out of scope)

(E) It's possible that someone might believe this, but the passage does not provide any information to indicate that conditions were once very different. (Out of scope)

4. **It can be inferred from the passage that scientists would be more likely to suspect that Mars once held life if there were evidence of which of the following features?**

    (A) Carbon dioxide oceans

    (B) Celestial radiation and solar wind

    (C) High daily level of sunlight reaching the planet's surface

    (D) Volcanic eruptions

    (E) A significant global magnetic field

This is an inference question. Both paragraphs discuss characteristics that are possible indicators of life. Because there are so many, go straight to the answers and try to find them in the passage. But first, remind yourself that the passage also discusses characteristics that are incompatible with life. Read carefully!

(A) The second paragraph mentions that carbon dioxide oceans, rather than water, might be responsible for certain land forms, and the passage makes clear that water is an important indicator of possible life. Carbon dioxide oceans, then, would weaken the evidence for water presence, and so would *not* increase the chances of life. (Direct contradiction)

(B) The first paragraph mentions celestial radiation and solar wind in the context of a scenario in which there is not life. (Direct contradiction)

(C) You might posit that abundant sunlight would improve the odds of life, but the passage does not provide any information about this. (Out of scope)

(D) The passage does not provide any information about volcanic eruptions. (Out of scope)

(E) CORRECT. The first paragraph indicates that Mars, unlike Earth, does *not* have a substantial global magnetic field and presents this information as a negative in the debate about life on Mars. The implication, then, is that a global magnetic field would be positive evidence in favor of life on Mars.

Passage N: Fossils

In archaeology, as in the physical sciences, new discoveries frequently undermine accepted findings and give rise to new theories. This trend can be seen in the reaction to the
(5) recent discovery of a set of 3.3-million-year old fossils in Ethiopia, the remains of the earliest well-preserved child ever found. The fossilized child was estimated to be about 3 years old at death, female, and a member
(10) of the *Australopithecus afarensis* species. The *afarensis* species, a major human ancestor, lived in Africa from earlier than 3.7 million to 3 million years ago. "Her completeness, antiquity, and age at death make this find
(15) unprecedented in the history of paleoanthropology," said Zeresenay Alemseged, a noted paleoanthropologist. Other scientists said that the discovery could reconfigure conceptions about the lives and capacities of these
(20) early humans.

Prior to this discovery, it had been thought that the *afarensis* species had abandoned the arboreal habitat of its ape cousins. However, while the lower
(25) limbs of this fossil supported findings that *afarensis* walked upright, its gorilla-like arms and shoulders suggested that it retained the ability to swing through trees. This has initiated a reexamination
(30) of many accepted theories of early human development. Also, the presence of a hyoid bone, a rarely preserved bone in the larynx that supports muscles of the throat, has had a tremendous impact on
(35) theories about the origins of speech. The fossil bone is primitive and more similar to that of apes than to that of humans, but it is the first hyoid found in such an early human-related
(40) species.

Sample passage map (yours will likely differ):

① *new disc --> undermine old*
   lead to new theories
      eg: child fossil
② *2 things that changed w/ disc of child*
   walking/limbs
   speech/hyoid

The point (articulate to yourself): New discoveries change old ideas and give rise to new theories. (Example: archaeology)

1. The primary purpose of the passage is to

    (A) discuss a controversial scientific discovery

    (B) contrast varying theories of human development

    (C) support a general contention with a specific example

    (D) argue for the importance of a particular field of study

    (E) refute a popular misconception

This is a primary purpose question. Glance at your map and remind yourself of the point before you go to the answers.

(A) The passage does not indicate that the discovery was in any way controversial. (Out of scope)

(B) The passage does discuss how certain theories about early human development have changed over time, but this is secondary to the point of the passage: that new discoveries can knock out old theories and give rise to new ones. (True but not right)

(C) CORRECT. The first sentence of the passage makes an overall contention. The rest of the passage provides a specific example to support that contention.

(D) The author uses the field of archaeology as an example to make a broader point that applies to other fields as well (the first sentence also mentions physical sciences). The author does not make a case about the importance of archaeology (or any other field) specifically. (Out of scope)

(E) The passage does indicate that, prior to the discovery mentioned, scientists had had a different theory about where and how *afarensis* lived, but this was not necessarily a popular misconception, merely an earlier scientific theory. In addition, this is a detail, not the point of the overall passage. (Out of scope)

2. The passage quotes Zeresenay Alemseged in order to

    (A) qualify the main idea of the first paragraph

    (B) provide contrast to the claims of other scientists

    (C) support the theory regarding the linguistic abilities of the *afarensis* species

    (D) support the stated significance of the discovery

    (E) provide a subjective opinion that is refuted in the second paragraph

The *in order to* language indicates that this is a specific purpose (why) question. Why did the author quote Alemseged in paragraph one?

"Her completeness, antiquity, and age at death make this find unprecedented in the history of paleoanthropology," said Zeresenay Alemseged, a noted paleoanthropologist. Other scientists said that the discovery could reconfigure conceptions about the lives and capacities of these early humans (lines 13–20).

The author is trying to use this example to support the point that discoveries can give rise to new theories. Alemseged's quote reinforces the idea that the discovery of this set of fossils is extremely significant (as does the mention of the other scientists afterwards).

(A) To qualify a piece of information is to limit or diminish it. Alemseged's quote reinforces the point, quite the opposite. (Direct contradiction)

(B) Alemseged's quote goes along with the ideas of the scientists mentioned after him. Although this discovery might undermine earlier ideas, no claims from earlier scientists are presented. (Direct contradiction)

(C) Linguistic abilities are mentioned at the end of the second paragraph, but Alemseged's quote is about the general significance of the find and it doesn't provide any support for a particular theory. (Mix-up)

(D) CORRECT. This choice matches the answer predicted above.

(E) Alemseged's quote is in line with the point; his opinion is reinforced, not refuted, by the second paragraph. (Direct contradiction)

3. It can be inferred from the passage's description of the discovery of the fossil hyoid bone that

(A) *Australopithecus afarensis* was capable of speech

(B) the discovered hyoid bone is less primitive than the hyoid bone of apes

(C) the hyoid bone is necessary for speech

(D) the discovery of the hyoid bone necessitated the reexamination of prior theories

(E) the hyoid bone was the most important fossil found at the site

This is an inference question. The hyoid bone was mentioned in the second paragraph:

This has initiated a reexamination of many accepted theories of early human development. Also, the presence of a hyoid bone, a rarely preserved bone in the larynx that supports muscles of the throat, has had a tremendous impact on theories about the origins of speech (lines 29–35).

Each example is used to bolster the idea that significant new discoveries can result in new theories. This latest discovery, the hyoid bone, had *a tremendous impact* (line 34) on the prior theories; in other words, the prior theories had to be reexamined (and possibly updated?) in light of this new information.

(A) This is tempting but goes too far. The passage related the hyoid to speech but does not provide information as to whether *afarensis* could actually speak. (Out of scope)

(B) Check the last sentence of the paragraph. Tricky! The sentence calls the bone primitive and similar to that of apes, but does not say that it is less primitive than the ones found in apes. (Out of scope)

(C) The passage does connect the hyoid bone to speech, but does not provide information that would imply that the bone is *necessary*. (Extreme)

(D) CORRECT. Leading into the hyoid example, the passage talks about discoveries leading to a reexamination of many accepted theories. The passage then says that the hyoid discovery has had a *tremendous impact* (line 34) on prior theories. The implication is that the hyoid discovery has also resulted in a reexamination of those prior theories.

(E) The discovery of the hyoid was certainly important, but the passage provides no information about which discovery was the most important. (Extreme)

4. Each of the following is cited as a reason that the fossils discovered in Ethiopia were important EXCEPT

   (A) the fact that the remains were those of a child

   (B) the age of the fossils

   (C) the location of the discovery

   (D) the presence of a bone not usually discovered

   (E) the intact nature of the fossils

The question indicates that four of the answers *are* mentioned in the passage, so this is a detail EXCEPT question. Most of the passage discusses fossil discoveries, so go straight to the first answer choice and try to find it in the passage.

(A) True. Alemseged's quote indicates that the *age at death* was important (lines 13–16).

(B) True. Alemseged's quote indicates that the *antiquity* of the bones was important (line 14).

(C) CORRECT. While the geographic location of the discovery is given in the passage (and the question) to indicate which bones are being discussed, it is false that the location was cited as a reason that the fossils were important.

(D) True. The hyoid example indicates that the bone is *rarely preserved* (line 37), and that it was the *first hyoid found in such an early human-related species* (lines 38–40). Because the discovery had such a tremendous impact, the discovery was important.

(E) True. Alemseged's quote indicates that the *completeness* of the bones was important (line 13).

5. The impact of the discovery of the hyoid bone in the field of archaeology is most closely analogous to which of the following situations?

(A) The discovery and analysis of cosmic rays lend support to a widely accepted theory of the origin of the universe.

(B) The original manuscript of a deceased nineteenth-century author confirms ideas about the development of an important work of literature.

(C) The continued prosperity of a state-run economy stirs debate in the discipline of macro-economics.

(D) Newly revealed journal entries by a prominent Civil War era politician lead to a questioning of certain accepted historical interpretations about the conflict.

(E) Research into the mapping of the human genome gives rise to nascent applications of individually tailored medicines.

This is an unusual question that does not fall into one of the common categories. The question is asking you to make an analogy to the situation presented in the passage. You may or may not see a question like this on the test.

The hyoid is mentioned in the second paragraph, so read the appropriate text and ask yourself what the *impact of the discovery* was. Then examine the answers to find a match.

The bone was the first hyoid found for this species and it had a *tremendous impact on theories about the origins of speech* (lines 34–35). Find a similar situation in the answers.

(A) and (B) The hyoid discovery led to a reexamination of the existing theory; it did not *support ... a widely accepted theory* or *confirm ideas.*

(C) The hyoid discovery inserted an important new piece of information into the conversation; this choice does not mention anything about new information or evidence.

(D) CORRECT. The hyoid discovery, like the newly revealed journal entries in this choice, led to questioning of certain interpretations or theories.

(E) The hyoid discovery had an impact on previously formulated theories. This choice does not address previous applications or theories.

6

Passage O: Chaos Theory

Around 1960, mathematician Edward Lorenz found unexpected behavior in apparently simple equations representing atmospheric air flows. Whenever he reran his model with (5) the same inputs, different outputs resulted, although the model lacked any random elements. Lorenz realized that tiny rounding errors in the initial data mushroomed over time, leading to erratic results. His findings (10) marked a seminal moment in the development of chaos theory, which, despite its name, has little to do with randomness.

Lorenz's experiment was one of the first to demonstrate conclusively that unpredict- (15) ability can arise from deterministic equations, which do not involve chance outcomes. In order to understand this phenomenon, first consider the non-chaotic system of two poppy seeds placed in a round bowl. As the seeds (20) roll to the bowl's center, a position known as a point attractor, the distance between the seeds shrinks. If, instead, the bowl is flipped over, two seeds placed on top will roll away from each other. Such a system, while still not (25) technically chaotic, enlarges initial differences in position.

Chaotic systems, such as a machine mixing bread dough, are characterized by both attraction and repulsion. As the dough is (30) stretched, folded, and pressed back together, any poppy seeds sprinkled in are inter-mixed seemingly at random. But this randomness is illusory. In fact, the poppy seeds are captured by "strange attrac- (35) tors," staggeringly complex pathways whose tangles appear accidental but are in fact determined by the system's fundamental equations.

During the dough-kneading process, (40) two poppy seeds positioned next to each other eventually go their separate ways. Any early divergence or measurement error is repeatedly amplified by the mixing until the position of any seed becomes (45) effectively unpredictable. It is this "sensitive dependence on initial conditions" and not true randomness that generates unpredictability in chaotic systems, of which one example may be the Earth's (50) weather. According to the popular interpretation of the "Butterfly Effect," a butterfly flapping its wings causes hurricanes. A better understanding is that the butterfly causes uncertainty about the (55) precise state of the air. This microscopic uncertainty grows until it encompasses even hurricanes. Few meteorologists believe that we will ever be able to predict rain or shine for a particular day years in (60) the future.

Sample passage map (yours will likely differ):

1. *Lorenz: diff results from rounding errors --> chaos theory (not random)*
2. *non-chaotic: bowl and poppy seeds*
3. *chaotic: mixing bowl and dough attract, repulse*
4. *not random, just depends on initial conditions butterfly*

The point (articulate to yourself): Lorenz discovered something about chaos theory (which is not really about randomness). Non-chaotic systems are predictable. Chaotic systems increase initial differences, so even though they are not actually random, they are hard to predict.

1. The primary purpose of this passage is to

    (A) explain how non-random systems can produce unpredictable results

    (B) trace the historical development of a scientific theory

    (C) distinguish one theory from its opposite

    (D) describe the spread of a technical model from one field of study to others

    (E) contrast possible causes of weather phenomena

This is a primary purpose question. Glance at your map and remind yourself of the point before you go to the answers.

(A) CORRECT. The passage does explain how chaotic (*non-random*) systems aren't actually predictable.

(B) The passage does discuss some of Lorenz's contributions to chaos theory, but the passage does not trace the entire historical development of the theory. (Out of scope)

(C) Only one theory (chaos theory) is mentioned in the passage. The passage does contrast two systems (non-chaotic and chaotic, but these are not both theories, nor is the overall point to contrast these two systems. (Out of scope)

(D) The passage does not discuss multiple fields of study. (Out of scope)

(E) The end of the passage does mention the weather, but there is no mention of different possible causes of weather phenomena. Even if there were, this would be detail, not the point. (Out of scope)

2. According to the passage, what is true about poppy seeds in bread dough, once the dough has been thoroughly mixed?

    (A) They have been individually stretched and folded over, like miniature versions of the entire dough.

    (B) They are scattered in random clumps throughout the dough.

    (C) They are accidentally caught in tangled objects called strange attractors.

    (D) They are bound to regularly dispersed patterns of point attractors.

    (E) They are in positions dictated by the underlying equations that govern the mixing process.

6

The language *according to the passage* indicates that this is a detail question. The bread dough concept is introduced in the third paragraph and continued in the fourth paragraph. Start with the third paragraph:

> As the dough is stretched, folded, and pressed back together, any poppy seeds sprinkled in are intermixed seemingly at random. But this randomness is illusory. In fact, the poppy seeds are captured by "strange attractors," staggeringly complex pathways whose tangles appear accidental but are in fact determined by the system's fundamental equations (lines 29–32).

After the dough is mixed, then, the seeds have separated based on some equations, but it's not possible to predict how. See whether there's a match in the answers; if not, try the fourth paragraph.

(A) The paragraph indicates that the dough is stretched and folded over, not the seeds. (Mix-up)

(B) The paragraph specifically indicates that the movement is *not* random. (Direct contradiction)

(C) "Strange attractor" is a technical name for a complex, tangled pathway. There are no tangled objects. Moreover, there is nothing accidental about the movement. (Mix-up)

(D) The seeds are not in regularly dispersed patterns; the patterns are so complex that the outcome is *seemingly at random* (line 32). Later, in the fourth paragraph, the passage makes clear that the final positions are not predictable (and therefore not regularly dispersed) even though they are actually governed by equations. (Out of scope)

(E) CORRECT. The final sentence of the third paragraph indicates that the system's fundamental equations determine the final position of the poppy seeds.

3. According to the passage, the rounding errors in Lorenz's model

    (A) rendered the results unusable for the purposes of scientific research

    (B) were deliberately included to represent tiny fluctuations in atmospheric air currents

    (C) had a surprisingly large impact over time

    (D) were at least partially expected, given the complexity of the actual atmosphere

    (E) shrank to insignificant levels during each trial of the model

The language *according to the passage* indicates that this is a detail question. The first paragraph introduces Lorenz's model and the rounding errors:

> Edward Lorenz found unexpected behavior in apparently simple equations representing atmospheric air flows. Whenever he reran his model with the same inputs, different outputs resulted—although the model lacked any random elements. Lorenz realized that tiny rounding errors in his analog computer mushroomed over time, leading to erratic results (lines 1–9).

The rounding errors were tiny at first but mushroomed (got much larger) over time, such that the final results of seemingly similar starting points could be quite different.

(A) The passage does not indicate whether Lorenz was still able to use the results for his purposes. If anything, the errors led to a positive, not negative, result: the erratic results led to *a seminal moment in the development of chaos theory* (lines 10–11). (Out of scope)

(B) Lorenz did not deliberately include the rounding errors. At first, he did not realize they were present and couldn't understand why he kept getting different results. (Direct contradiction)

(C) CORRECT. The rounding errors were so tiny that Lorenz did not notice them immediately, but they *mushroomed over time* until they produced different results even with seemingly the same inputs. The passage describes this behavior as *unexpected*.

(D) The rounding errors were simply computer errors; the passage does not indicate that they resulted from the complexity of the atmosphere. (Mix-up)

(E) On the contrary, the rounding errors grew a great deal, or *mushroomed*, over time. (Direct contradiction)

4. **The passage mentions each of the following as an example or potential example of a chaotic or non-chaotic system EXCEPT**

(A) a dough-mixing machine

(B) atmospheric weather patterns

(C) poppy seeds placed on top of an upside-down bowl

(D) poppy seeds placed in a right-side-up bowl

(E) fluctuating butterfly flight patterns

The question indicates that four of the answers *are* mentioned in the passage, so this is a detail EXCEPT question. The entire passage talks about both chaotic and non-chaotic systems, so it's not possible to formulate an answer in advance. Go straight to the first answer choice and try to find it in the passage.

(A) True. The first sentence of the third paragraph indicates that a *machine mixing bread dough* (lines 27–28) is an example of a chaotic system.

(B) True. The fourth paragraph mentions one possible example of a chaotic system as *Earth's weather* (lines 48–50).

(C) and (D) True. The second paragraph describes the poppy seed examples as non-chaotic systems (lines 18–19).

(E) CORRECT. While it is true that the passage discusses a *butterfly flapping its wings* (line 52), it is false that the passage mentions anything about butterfly flight patterns.

6

GO BEYOND BOOKS.
TRY A FREE CLASS NOW.

IN-PERSON COURSE

Find a GMAT course near you and attend the first session free, no strings attached. You'll meet your instructor, learn how the GMAT is scored, review strategies for Data Sufficiency, dive into Sentence Correction, and gain insights into a wide array of GMAT principles and strategies.

**Find your city at
manhattanprep.com/gmat/classes**

ONLINE COURSE

Enjoy the flexibility of prepping from home or the office with our online course. Your instructor will cover all the same content and strategies as an in-person course, while giving you the freedom to prep where you want. Attend the first session free to check out our cutting-edge online classroom.

**See the full schedule at
manhattanprep.com/gmat/classes**

GMAT® INTERACT™

GMAT Interact is a comprehensive self-study program that is fun, intuitive, and driven by you. Each interactive video lesson is taught by an expert instructor and can be accessed on your computer or mobile device. Lessons are personalized for you based on the choices you make.

**Try 5 full lessons for free at
manhattanprep.com/gmat/interact**

Not sure which is right for you? Try all three! Or give us a call and we'll help you figure out which program fits you best.

Toll-Free U.S. Number (800) 576-4628 | **International** 001 (212) 721-7400 | **Email** gmat@manhattanprep.com

PREP MADE PERSONAL

Whether you want quick coaching
in a particular GMAT subject area
or a comprehensive study plan developed
around your goals, we've got you covered.
Our expert, 99th percentile GMAT tutors
can help you hit your top score.

CHECK OUT THESE REVIEWS FROM MANHATTAN PREP TUTORING STUDENTS.

CALL OR EMAIL US AT **800-576-4628** OR **GMAT@MANHATTANPREP.COM**
FOR INFORMATION ON RATES AND TO GET PAIRED WITH YOUR GMAT TUTOR.